Down... But NOT Out

Down... But NOT Out

Why life gets most of us down – and how to get yourself back up

Mat Desforges

Cherish
EDITIONS

First published in Great Britain 2021 by Cherish Editions

Cherish Editions is a trading style of Shaw Callaghan Ltd & Shaw Callaghan
23 USA, INC.

The Foundation Centre

Navigation House, 48 Millgate, Newark

Nottinghamshire NG24 4TS UK

www.triggerhub.org

Text Copyright © 2021 Mat Desforges

British Library Cataloguing in Publication Data

A CIP catalogue record for this book is available upon request

from the British Library

ISBN: 978-1-913615-21-5

This book is also available in the following eBook formats:

ePUB: 978-1-913615-22-2

Mat Desforges has asserted his right under the Copyright,
Design and Patents Act 1988 to be identified as the author of this work

Cover design by More Visual

Typeset by Lapiz Digital Services

This book is for everyone who feels low at some time, whatever the reason.
It is also for the lucky few who don't feel like this. Hopefully they can understand, support and be there for the rest of us.
The sun does come out again.

CONTENTS

PROLOGUE

There are times when I feel sad. I can get low. I can be stressed. The smallest of life's setbacks can feel like disasters. The easiest tasks feel like massive, unachievable obstacles. I can get no joy from joyful situations. I can simply not care. I can feel doom and feel doomed.

Some people may label it depression; perhaps it is. But, more likely, it is just low feelings. Those low feelings that I believe most of us experience at some point in our lives.

Maybe you feel the same. If you do, maybe I feel less low than you do… or maybe more. Who knows? I am probably somewhere in the middle. Perhaps. But one thing I am confident about is that I am not alone in my low feelings, and that many, many people face similar challenges. Perhaps you do, too.

Don't put this book down because you think that it is going to be sad or depressing. It is not. Well, okay, some of it is, maybe. Overwhelmingly, it should be uplifting and help to create some joy. It should provide some reasons for you to move on from the sad times to happier feelings.

Fortunately, my low points aren't there all the time. In fact, they are probably there a minority of the time. I can feel happiness. I can feel genuine joy. I can be in the moment with absolute focus and living life to the full.

But those low moments do exist, and they can be tough.

When I recently went through a particularly low period, my brain shouted more loudly than usual, "Enough is enough." I had an "episode", as I call it in this book. Not a major breakdown, but it was serious. My brain let me know it was really struggling. Fortunately, I listened. I took the time and I assessed what was wrong. I sought help, analysed the reasons for my low moods and tried to come up with sustainable solutions.

This book is a summary of that specific low time, the potential reasons behind it and my solutions for getting through that episode and any future ones.

One thing in particular that has struck me is that the reasons for my moods are merely the inevitabilities of being human – of just living. Equally, the solutions for my challenges come through living as well, and therefore they are not impossible or unachievable.

Perhaps that is why almost all of us, to some degree, have some low moods. We are all alive, and that fact alone is enough to trigger some stress and low feelings. We all get them, to some extent.

Equally, and probably more importantly, we also all have some access to the solutions.

We feel pain and low moods because we are human beings: the reason.

*We can go some way to heal that pain and those low moods by being **human**: the solution.*

This is the essence of what we are and what we do – humans and being. But perhaps by upgrading "being" to "living", we can heal those low moods. It is through really living that we can solve those problems.

The low moods caused by being human and alive can be lifted by being human and living – by talking, interacting, walking, working, running, breathing… anything we do, whether it's because we like to or because we have to.

By being human. By just being.

PART ONE
THE FALLING

THIS IS NOT GOOD; IN FACT, THIS IS V. V. BAD

"I want to buy a router," I calmly announced in the local telecommunications shop one Tuesday lunchtime, late in the autumn. Just another ordinary transaction on an ordinary day, in an ordinary shop, by an ordinary person. It was me about to buy the router, and it was me about to have a life-changing experience. But, equally, it could have been you – or anyone.

"No problem, sir. Please just take a seat over there and one of our assistants will be with you shortly," replied the young, trendy-looking man behind the welcome desk as he pointed at some comfy chairs at the back of the shop.

That familiar irritation of being left to wait unnecessarily brewed up inside me. Nothing major, but it was there. The risk of "red mist" descending was here. I needed to be careful.

"Just chill," my brain was telling me. "It won't be long."

"Please, I just want a router. I phoned yesterday. It's £100. Please, just sell me a router," I firmly, but calmly, announced.

"It's not that simple sir, there are different options to discuss, payment plans and the router needs…" the assistant continued, but I was starting to feel weird. I looked at the assistant for a few seconds, and he again pointed to the comfy chair area.

The red mist wasn't there, but something else was happening, something I hadn't experienced before.

My brain wasn't telling me very much by now. It had almost gone into slow motion – like when you film in slo-mo on your phone. Everything was clear and slow, but I was the viewer watching that film.

I couldn't change what was happening; I was just a passenger in my own body for the next few moments.

I froze, I looked at him again, then shuffled to the chairs. All in slo-mo.

Or was I going at normal speed? I couldn't tell. And I couldn't control it.

I was unable to speak, unable to further state why I didn't want to wait. Then my mind went blank, but at the same time was completely full. I could see everything, but I could control almost nothing. And everything around me still felt like it was in slow motion.

This was no longer normal. This was not me. This was not an ordinary day and an ordinary transaction.

***

I am about to try and explain a bizarre set of feelings, which will be full of contradictions. At that moment, I was not aware of what was about to unfold. An innocuous encounter in a telecommunications shop was about to trigger my brain into some sort of overload. Some may call it the straw that broke the camel's back, but – whatever it's called, here's what happened, as far as I can remember.

As I said, my mind was blank but utterly full. I found myself sitting on the bright, comfy chair. The details were crystal clear. I could feel every part of my body that was in contact with the seat and my feet on the floor – but not in a normal way.

I could sense the subtleties of the different position each foot was in, the tiny difference in angle of each foot on the floor. Further up, I could feel the sensation as I sat and exactly where my lower back was positioned in the chair. My upper back was squashed more than my lower back, leaving me slightly hunched. My neck was gently touching the top of the chair and my head was resting on the head rest. My forearms on each armrest were slightly different, with a different sense of pressure on each. I could feel it all, every last sensation, in a way that I had never previously experienced.

My eyes took in every detail of my surroundings. What each person in the shop was wearing, the colour and texture of the walls and carpet. It was like I had 20:20 vision and was able to see a full 180-degree sweep with no blind spots in my peripheral vision.

At the same time, every tiny sound was amplified and detailed. I could hear the assistants talking to other customers in the distance. I could hear every word across a large room. Outside, I heard the cars go past on the street.

My body was in sensory overload, and I felt, saw, smelt, heard and could almost taste every aspect of the shop.

The movements around me meant everything and nothing. I don't know what would have happened had an external catastrophe – a fire or an explosion or a robbery – enveloped the shop that day. We all like to think that in such an event we would act calmly, swiftly and heroically. But that day would not have been my day.

It is entirely possible that I would have just sat there in a trance-like state. The other customers would have rushed out and been unable to fathom why this totally normal-looking bloke was just rooted to the spot. The investigators later would have scratched their heads, unable to explain my inertia.

But I digress. Fortunately, there was no external catastrophe. The only catastrophe was in my head.

While I was in this heightened state of awareness mixed with total inertia, I was totally disconnected from everything around me. I was unable to move, I was rooted to the seat. I couldn't move my head, and I couldn't speak. My brain was operating in slow motion.

The realization that I was not in control hit me. Or was I in control? I couldn't move to determine whether I was or wasn't. As I said, the feeling was full of contradictions.

Describing it now is hard. To the outsider looking in, it probably looked like nothing – just another impatient, moody customer. "Get over yourself," is probably what you would have been thinking. The experience to the outsider would have been indiscernible. But to me, within me, it was one of the strangest and most intense experiences I had ever felt.

Then it became as though I was outside my body looking in. After the event, I described the sensation as being "detached" from my body and mind. I was aware exactly of who I was, where I was and what I was doing, but it was as if I was witnessing it as a third party.

In my head, I was calm yet calculating. I was aware, but totally drifting.

I sat motionless for ten, perhaps fifteen minutes, I am still not sure. Maybe it was only five. Maybe it was thirty. Time stood still, or was it racing away? It was unclear to me.

I no longer really remembered why I was there or even where I was; I was just somewhere, sat down. And while I was sat down, I felt safe somehow; I didn't have to do anything or interact with anyone, I could just be there.

As the intensity of the feelings grew, the more still I sat.

Then I remembered what I was there for. My mind clicked into another state – not normality, just quiet determination. I was determined to get that damned router. We had been without Wi-Fi for a week. No Wi-Fi for a week! Secretly, I had loved it at the start – the peace and quiet, the disconnect from the world.

But then the reality of being unable to do anything sunk in. There had been evenings trying to configure another router. The kids had moaned about the lack of Wi-Fi. And, frankly, it was making life tricky. The kids were grouchy, my wife was getting annoyed, and I was cheesed off with the fact nothing worked without Wi-Fi. My early thoughts of getting back to basics had been replaced with the frustration and annoyance of when something doesn't work and you just can't damn well fix it!

This shop had the router I needed. I knew they did because I had called ahead. They had said to come in. They could sell it to me. I wanted it – NO! – I NEEDED the router.

In my head, I was moving away from my bizarre yet slightly serene earlier state and I was screaming, "LET ME HAVE THE FXXCKING ROUTER!"

I went back to the desk and robotically repeated, "I am here to buy a router. I have been left waiting. Please SELL me a ROUTER."

All I could offer was the shortest of sentences. I didn't shout, I was measured and abnormally emphasised the words in my sentence. The young trendy guy looked concerned, probably as a result of my tone, and assured me with a strained look in his eye that an assistant would be with me very soon.

He just wanted me gone. I was turning into his problem, and he probably had enough problems already. And he was right – someone was about to help me – I was called forward.

My detached state continued as I walked forward to see a staff member. Part of me wanted to run, to escape from the shop. I could probably smash a few things on the way out, shout a few obscenities – go out in a blaze of "screw your router" glory.

But another part of me was focused, with steely determination, on the purchase.

The assistant quizzed me and I gave monosyllabic answers. This was a dull transaction for a dull product, and I was giving off the air of someone who was extremely bored and very disconnected.

I don't know how many questions there were, but I think it was a five- or ten-minute encounter. I knew what I was saying in reply, but I was unable to offer any more than the barest of information. It was like my brain was on autopilot and I couldn't override it. The conversation continued in a stilted way, as if someone else was talking for me. I was just outside looking in and hearing someone else answer the questions.

As I said, this is not exciting stuff to describe. But to me it was intense and colourful, yet grey at the same time. My mind was behaving really weirdly, and I wasn't in control. There was nothing I could do to change what was happening.

I may have been coming across "too cool for school", as though I really didn't give a damn and held the shop and the assistant in contempt. I hope I wasn't rude, but in reality I know I was. At the time I really didn't care – I didn't have the capacity to care. To them, I probably just looked like a bit of an idiot.

I was cool, but in a cold way. The staff member looked at me and sensed something was up. I don't know what he thought, but I guess it was something along the lines of, "I want this weird guy out of here asap."

I gave him my bank card. He gave me a box. I didn't check what was in it, but the box was mine. Maybe it had a router in it. Maybe it had some other random item. To be honest, my mind was acting so weirdly I didn't care by then. I was out.

My strange state continued. I was still in slow motion. I couldn't speed up and I couldn't slow down. My legs were moving, I was walking, but I was unable to control the speed or the direction. I just walked. I knew I had to get somewhere safe.

I was stressed – but calm, utterly calm.

I walked to a safe place and sat down. *Deep breaths. Take it easy.* Slowly, I seemed to return to some sense of normality. But my overriding feeling was, "What was that? What had happened?"

This was not good.

This was very, very bad.

I was out of the shop and calming down. This could happen to anyone. We all go shopping, and most of us cope. But maybe the last time you were in a shop, the person next to you was going through what I had just gone through.

It could have happened anywhere – on the bus, on a train, in work, at the cinema, in a restaurant. Anywhere. And that is the point. It could happen to anyone, anywhere. To your husband, your wife, your child or parent. To you.

You and me.

ENOUGH IS ENOUGH

So, what had happened?

I don't fly fighter jets and I don't work in a dangerous environment, but even so the best analogy I can come up with for what happened that day comes from the opening scene of the 1980s film *Top Gun*: our hero, Maverick, is doing some heroic stuff, cool and calm, in control, up in the air with the Russian MIG fighter jets on his back. While in the other jet was a guy called Cougar, who was being far from cool and far from in control. Remember the scene? Cougar was shaking, he couldn't focus, he was done for.

Well, guess what? I was Cougar.

Cougar couldn't land the plane on the aircraft carrier, and it was not looking good. I felt that I was at the stage that Cougar probably was just before he "lost it" on that final mission. I was aware that something wasn't right, that something was going to go very wrong. I was on the edge, the brink. My body and mind were warning me, and I had to listen.

Hopefully you can smile at the analogy, yet get a little sense of the despair and hopelessness I felt. Although, if you haven't seen the film it won't mean much!

Basically, I was a mess. My life was out of control. And I was feeling the painful mental and physical consequences.

The reality was that I was just a normal person doing normal things. I could feel relatively strong, happy and resilient most of the time. But I was also struggling. And as a result, I could feel weak, morose and vulnerable.

It was not a happy place, and I had had a wake-up call.

I foresaw (and in the following days I shared these thoughts with others) that there were two possible scenarios from here:

- I carry on and "crack" or "break" – whatever that actually is. But I figured that whatever it was would be messy for many people. It wouldn't help me, my family or my work. I thought that waiting for that moment and then trying to come back from it was going to be a whole lot harder for everyone.
- I shout out now and get help. I didn't know what that would entail. I didn't know what others would think. And I certainly didn't know if it would do any good. It also scared me – to own up to what had happened, to own up to the fact that life was not fine and dandy. It was far from that.

Despite the unknowns and my concerns, I was determined to choose the second option.

According to my doctor, who I saw soon after the episode, I'd experienced "dissociation" in the telecom shop.

That doesn't sound too bad, I thought to myself. *This guy knows what it is so presumably he can help.* But then I recalled the depth of the negative feelings I had experienced. It was a place I had not been to before and it was one that scared me. But at least there was a name for it.

A quick Google search describes dissociation as "A break in how your mind handles information. You may feel disconnected from your thoughts, feelings, memories and surroundings. It can affect your sense of identity and perception of time." The definition continues, "Experts believe this is a technique your mind uses to protect you from the full impact of the upsetting experience you had."[1]

I didn't know about dissociation on that fateful Tuesday; I had never even heard of it. But with hindsight it did vaguely ring true, and I could recognize some, if not all, of the descriptors. At least I now had a label for this.

Maybe my doctor was correct, maybe not, but I had something to go on. That provided some comfort.

---

1 Source: webmd.com

As I read more detail on Google (using Google for medical diagnoses is, as we all know, dangerous and risky, yet we all do it!), I learnt more. It talked about dissociation being as simple as daydreaming. *All good*, I thought. But then it went further and discussed post-traumatic stress disorders and unresolved childhood traumas.

This new term that I could now throw around was just a generic term for a complex and varied phenomenon. It was like saying, "I need some money, so I'll go and get a job." But what job? A pilot or a policeman? A brain surgeon or a shop assistant? Or like saying, "I'm hungry, I'll cook some food." But what? Steak or vegan pie? Chips or salad?

The new word helped, but I realized I was at the tip of an iceberg. The reasons for me feeling like this were complex, and the solutions suddenly seemed much harder.

***

Going back to that Tuesday – the day of the episode – I calmed down, eventually returned to work, quickly tied up some loose ends (basically grabbed my stuff), made my excuses and headed home. This needed some thought.

Normally, I am not one to break down in a shop, not the kind of person to fly off the handle (unless really provoked when I was much younger), and I had certainly not experienced anything like I had felt that day.

Sure, I may lack patience sometimes if faced with the odd excessively stressful event, and certain things may piss me off and get me annoyed. Isn't this the same for everyone? The Dalai Lama is a one off – the rest of us mortals get annoyed. So what?

But this was different, very different.

I knew I'd had a tough few days at work – okay, a tough few weeks – but nothing fundamentally different to many times before.

What seemed to have happened was a gradual ramping up of stresses and strains. When one negative thing would hit me, I could deal with it. Two or three negative things, the same – dealt with. Many people have demanding jobs and multiple stressful things can happen.

I am no exception and I am normally fine to deal with them. But what was different was my experience that Tuesday – when it seemed that my brain didn't deal with multiple stressful situations in the normal way. It seemed that my brain had reached its capacity.

Over the previous few months, I knew I had been low, perhaps verging on depressed, and I had that constant nagging doubt that I was far from fulfilled in my life. On one hand, my life was fine, but on the other hand, I was low and unhappy.

But my reaction that day had been extreme. On my journey home, I thought about the previous few months at work, about life in general and about other factors. I analysed, I probed, and I did some different thinking – much more honest thinking. I challenged the norm and dared to think differently.

I had a moment of clarity. With hindsight it was so obvious. Isn't that what moments of clarity are? I realized that my low feelings and the episode in the shop were the symptoms, and there were clearly other reasons and causes for these feelings. It wasn't a eureka moment, it was just obvious. By focusing on the symptoms of my problems and trying to deal with those, I had lost sight of the causes.

It was a great moment – daft as it sounds, I realized that I just had to sort out the reasons behind the symptoms and then they would ease. Instead of accepting that I was just feeling low and short-tempered, I knew I could try to solve what was making me low and short-tempered.

This realization brought some positive feelings in what was otherwise an altogether shitty day. I held on to that positive thought – it was hard, but I did it. The reality of low feelings is that you are in a hole – you can only see darkness and feel sides, so it's hard to escape. Any light is faint and seems impossibly out of reach. So, any glimmer of hope that I could perhaps get out of this was something to hold on to. I knew that the alternative was bad.

I continued to head for home, knowing what I had to do. I had to talk. I had to tell. I had to get some help. That Tuesday afternoon's episode had been my sign. My brain had been communicating with me and it was clearly shouting, "ENOUGH IS ENOUGH!" I was going to shout for help and I was going to make sure I got it.

WRITE IT DOWN

So that in essence is how this journey, this book, this way of thinking and this change in me started. To be honest, I am still working it all out (and I guess I will never truly work it out), but my intention is to try and articulate:

- The **reasons** why I felt like that – the triggers. (This was not due to the router! There was a complex set of contributing factors.)
- The **solutions** – discussions, advice, counselling and tools to deal with this type of stress and low mood.
- The **future,** and what it may hold if I adopt these solutions.

But why write all this down?

There were a number of reasons. Once my work and my doctor decided that I should have some time to deal with this situation, I suddenly had some spare time and I was determined to use it wisely. I wanted to use this experience for a positive change. Rather than see the episode as a negative event (which I most definitely did at the time and in the immediate aftermath), I now see it as a wake-up call and as a massive opportunity – an opportunity for me and for others.

Another reason is that I felt terrible, really terrible. Sitting here now, months after the event, I feel okay. But it's also very easy to cast my mind back and feel that pain again. Those low, negative, self-scathing thoughts I felt as I thought my life had fundamentally changed; I was in a bad place, stuck in a dark tunnel, unable to see any light.

Equally, I knew deep down that I was experiencing a "light" version of feeling stressed, low and verging on depressed. I knew a lot of other people had my symptoms multiplied by ten or a hundred. You hear of people with really acute depression – those who simply cannot function or interact or go outside. There are others suffering depression on top of having a really tough life. And you also hear of people experiencing all of those things.

As bad as I felt, I was also confident that I was not in that group of acutely depressed people with massive persistent challenges and tough, tough lives. And, for that, I felt lucky, very lucky. I couldn't pretend to be able to make sense of what acute depression is like, because it was another level to mine. I was in the bracket that I believe affects a much larger group of people – the masses who go about their lives with black clouds on many days but still function vaguely normally. I felt I could help this large group through trying to make sense of and documenting my experiences.

But why should my scribbles be any different to the next book on the shelf about life's problems and how we deal with them? You'll have seen them on the Internet, in the bookshops, in the papers, titles such as:

- "Self-help"
- "Life's fxxxed and how to deal with it"
- "Saying no"
- "How to meditate"
- "Mindfulness"
- "Find your true self"

And so on. All these books have their value. I get the concept – I am into that outlook, I am open-minded and appreciate the need to try to understand and improve myself. Yet I find that many of these books are a bit unappealing, or they don't fully answer my questions.

These books can be overly analytical and theoretical – too much like a work course on steroids – invariably written by someone with years of clinical experience; or the book is just too long to read. Many books are also about the real extremes of depression rather than people just generally feeling a bit shit, like I was, but trying to get on with life anyway.

Many of those other books are useful (I know they are, because I have read some), but I wanted more of a story – a story of a normal guy going through normal problems and having to deal with them via accessible and workable solutions.

I am no different from you. We are all broadly the same: the same genetics, the same physiology, essentially the same wiring. My problems, concerns and worries are no different from those of the next person. We are "uniquely un-unique".

If I can make some sense of my episode and my low feelings, start to understand the reasons behind them and the solutions to get through them, then not only can I channel this event into a positive change for me, but maybe others can be helped along the way.

That is the aim. Let's see how we go.

THE EARLY DAYS

After my experience in the telecommunications shop, I gradually started to feel better as the days went on. I took things a bit easier – I was off work and I focused more on myself. The immediate stressors had been eliminated. I felt pretty good... compared to where I had been a few days before!

The classic J-change curve definitely took shape. The J-curve is where after an immediate event you move down a curve, or you feel worse, then as time goes one you start to feel better – you are on an upward curve of feeling better. I had dipped, but then I soon jumped back up and felt better.

Hey, this is going to be okay, I thought to myself. But then things changed again.

I thought I was getting to grips with the issues, but apparently not. I soon slipped back into negative feelings. I felt as bad, perhaps worse, than I had, and some other dissociation events or moments took place. They were equally as intense, but I was learning to understand them more and knew that they would pass. The negative feelings were nothing particularly different to before, but when they are deep and multiple they can put you in a very low, lonely place – I was there.

I was irritable. The smallest little thing could throw me into some angry thoughts. One day, I made a call to pay a bill and the guy said they couldn't take payment over the phone at that time, and could I call back later?

Wow, did that annoy me and nearly push me backward?! I just wanted this tiny little job ticked off my list. I knew I could pay online, but that meant accessing the internet, finding account numbers, etc., when I was struggling to do even the smallest thing.

Another day, I was out for a bike ride on a cycle path and a lady quite politely said, "Could you cycle on the road?" *This is a bloody cycle path*, I fumed inside. I nearly went back and shouted to vent my frustration. Crikey, I was getting angry at anything. She was an old lady being polite for goodness sake!

The good part was that, in the main, I could control these moods. I would breathe deeply, remove myself from the situation, and try and put it into perspective. I had a new awareness that something was up and that I had to be careful. I felt I could do this – just – but I was getting a glimpse of how people who flip out must feel. It worried me that I could easily flip into doing something more serious. This real worry for my welfare, and that of others, intensified my desire to sort these problems out.

My sleeping got worse. I would wake in the early hours and worries and concerns would spin around my head for ages. Getting back to sleep was impossible. If lucky, I would slip off to sleep, but often it was minutes before I had to get up anyway. I was getting increasingly tired.

I then started having some more physical sensations of stress. I would have headaches and aching. My head would be woolly, unable to focus on even the simplest of things. I would be dazed, and people would talk to me and I wouldn't take much in.

Social situations started to worry me. I would see a group of people (many of whom I knew well and whose company I enjoyed) and I would avoid them. We had a social gathering we had to attend, and I found myself dipping into other rooms to get away from people. Other gatherings, I just avoided. I was hiding myself away.

The negative side of alcohol loomed its ugly head. Only briefly, thank goodness, as I was aware of the dangers. I remember once, many years before, being described as a "happy drunk". I was only ever a social drinker, and had had my fair share of enjoyable nights out and parties while under the influence. But nothing excessive and only at social occasions. I enjoyed the relaxing side of a beer and the enhanced and different social interaction and laughter that it could produce. But I had never experienced the negative side of alcohol in myself before. Sure, I had seen friends who could be aggressive or get down while drinking, but that had never happened to me. In my situation it wasn't aggression, it was just feeling low.

Then there was one party and one beer. Literally one beer. I felt the negative feelings really kick in. Like *really* kick in – it was as though I was on a helter-skelter and had just been pushed off the top. I wasn't aggressive or rowdy, but just collapsed into myself. I left the party. The next day I was exhausted and even more negative. I realized that even the slightest amount of alcohol had to be avoided.

I was back to lacking the desire to engage in activities or to realize the joy in little things.

The above is just a summary of some of the feelings I felt over the first few weeks after the episode. They weren't every minute of every day, and I had some happy times as well. But overall, I was negative and felt low.

One thing I realized early on though was that there was very likely going to be more dips. It was good to recognize this, and important to remember, even in those low times, that the general curve would hopefully be upwards.

So, why did the dips happen? Could I have avoided the double dip in the early weeks after the episode? What were the main reasons behind it?

In part, I think I was still learning what my main problems were. I was also trying to deal with problems I didn't truly understand and only using old strategies and old habits. These old strategies were to just take a bit of time out, avoid stressful situations but to keep busy and try and carry on with various projects – which, let's face it, had probably contributed to me being in that low place in the first instance!

I can probably best explain it as overload. I was used to having multiple problems and dealing with these by having multiple solutions all running at once. But now I had too many problems and I couldn't focus on anything.

I was rushing around, squeezing lots of things in, and jumping from one thing to the next. I was lacking focus as a result. I was just "doing" things – anything – just to feel I was busy (which I thought would help).

In those first few days and weeks I was compiling lists of things to do. These lists fell into different categories, such as: counselling; online help; resting; thinking about the problem; discussing with others; meeting people from work; doing some jobs at home that I had never had the time for; sport; walks in the fresh air; meditation – the list went on!

I was doing many of the right kind of things, but I was trying to do them all together! I was just rushing from one solution/activity to the next.

My impatience and inability to relax and take stock (again, all things that I feel had contributed to my negative feelings) were, yet again, getting the better of me. And I had more time to do these things now!! My days were busy, I was shattered, and I wasn't improving. I was very up and down.

This came to a head when I was looking at my lists and felt my stress and negativity rushing back. *But I have to do all these things to get better*, was all I thought. I then shared these feelings and lists with a couple of people and they looked at me with that knowing eye.

"Just stop," was what their facial expression was saying, but I couldn't see it. They had to spell it out. They told me to stop and to take a rest. A proper rest. This was going to take a while to resolve.

I had to do less. I had to focus on getting better and recovering from the brain overload I had experienced. A helpful message arrived from a friend who had been through a similar experience – it simply read, "rest and fresh air." It was a really helpful moment – sure those two things were on my list, and I knew I had to do them, but so were many other things and I was trying to do them all, every day!

On the same day I had another personal discovery. I was asked, "How do you relax?" I listed out many things, such as time with family, cycling, surfing and gardening. After a bit of discussion and reflection I realized that I wasn't relaxing, I was constantly "doing." I was just running from one activity to another. All my relaxing was an active pastime.

I think much of this led to my "double dip". I had been through a trauma after weeks and months of overload, and I needed to allow my body and mind to recover and to rest and heal. I still struggle to just relax for long periods, and I still like to do a lot. But I am aware of the need to truly relax, to take time for me, to not constantly be "doing."

I know the sayings, "soon this will pass", and "the clouds will part to reveal some blue sky", and "everything's just a phase", and I practice and preach these when I can. But I also now know the harsh reality that when you are feeling low there is little anyone can say to make you see those positive things and the fact that you will feel better in the end. It really is hard to dig yourself out of the hole.

But dig is what I had to do.

THE PROCESS

Everything seems to be a process these days. Sports teams talk about the process and how to refine it. Work is full of processes and about how to make them efficient and effective.

I felt I knew enough about the process, that is the journey, that I would need to take. As with any process, it was a case of breaking it down – thinking about what my desired end point was, and then going back to the start and taking one stage at a time; prioritising and not overloading and, most importantly, seeking help.

The night of my episode, my wife heard it all – the whole miserable day. I also set up a meeting for first thing the next day with my boss, and he heard it all too.

In simple terms, I felt I was at the stage just *before* a significant negative event – on a cliff edge. My episode had been a warning. I could see that if I carried on it wasn't going to end well; it was probably going to end in me going over the edge.

Over the next few days, I saw friends, had phone calls, saw the doctor, set up sessions with a counsellor, and sought assistance from the local health services. I was on my journey, working through the process; I was talking about the possible reasons behind the episode, as well as spending time alone considering the various triggers and factors.

I initially thought I had lots of possible reasons, and then the list contracted and then expanded again. I was determined not to leave any stone unturned, but to be open-minded that I may be coming up with reasons that weren't actually valid.

Through discussions with those close to me and with third parties, along with deep reflection, I thought I was getting closer to a valid list of reasons. I have no doubt the list is incomplete, but I was starting to understand the factors at play.

If the first stage of solving a problem is acknowledging it is there, then, Hallelujah – I was well on my way to first base.

I kept coming back to the likelihood that there were various factors at play, various reasons for feeling like this. Life is full of ups and downs, we have bad news and good news, positive experiences and negative experiences. I looked at the different factors and a couple of things struck me.

Firstly, I was aware that my life had ups and downs, and my mood followed these to some extent. If out of, say, ten key areas of my life, one or two were on a downward path then I could probably cope with this. It was okay to have a few downward areas as the other upward or stable areas made up for it. In those instances, I was generally happy.

But, when many areas of my life were on a downward turn, I got overloaded. Then I got low.

I didn't realize at the time leading up to my episode that there were multiple, simultaneous downward curves. I would just "fight fires", problem solve these stressful situations – I would analyse the issue and come up with a solution. What I didn't realize was that I was doing this in lots of areas. I was probably "down" in seven or eight out of ten areas.

If I had been able to acknowledge and to take account of the fact that all these downward spirals were happening together I would probably have thought, "Hey, no wonder I feel shitty."

Secondly, I was living close to maximum capacity in many areas of my life. Work, home, family, play, admin – I was juggling lots of balls in the air at the same time. I felt I was able to cope, but as soon as another ball got thrown in or one of the balls got bigger and trickier to catch then I struggled.

Another simple analogy is to look at all the areas of my life as if they were buckets. I had a few buckets and they were all pretty much full of water – at maximum or near to maximum capacity – and I could cope with that. However, if one bucket was emptied (perhaps I concluded a project at home or work), then I would quickly (and subconsciously) look to fill that bucket right back up again.

But then if some extra water got added to one of the buckets (an additional project at work or a new activity to do at home), then it would only take a tiny bit more water to make that bucket overflow. The overflowing water is a metaphor for my stress – I couldn't contain it. I couldn't empty the bucket or get a bigger bucket, so it just kept overflowing. I was losing control of the water, and I was losing control of my life.

Another way I looked at it was in terms of a machine. It doesn't really take much to make a well-oiled machine suddenly stop working. The human body is no different. Put a grain of sand in your eye or a small stone in your shoe. Both tiny, innocuous items against the power and complexity of the human body. But before long, the human body is going to have to stop and expel that stone or grain of sand. And from my experience our minds are not so different: little reasons can cause big problems. The good thing is that often these little challenges can be solved relatively quickly. The acknowledgment of the problem is the first challenge, and the solution can come soon after.

So, here follows my analysis of the buckets and causes of my stress and low moods which I was dealing with and why they were so full! Each bucket was a part of my life, and within it was the potential for negative feelings.

And while the contents of my buckets might be the same as those of the next guy on the bus, perhaps the difference is that I had taken the action of listing them, thinking about them, discussing them, and I was hell bent on turning them into solutions.

Solutions to get me out of the miserable place I found myself – and more than that, positive changes to get me into a better place and back to normal.

PART TWO
THE REASONS

INTRODUCTION

The reasons behind mental wellbeing seem to be massively complex. The research I have done into the subject and the brain itself has revealed layers and layers of complexity and theory. The finest neurologists and neuroscientists still don't seem to agree on how the brain really functions in many areas. So, my analysis of the reasons for my low feelings is bound to be lacking somewhat from a scientific perspective!

Yet, what I thought I could add was a balanced analysis of why *I* thought I was feeling like this. This involved a lot of soul searching with the help of others, and some serious thinking time.

Although it was tempting to also try some amateur psychology on myself and look back at my childhood and adolescence, I wanted to focus on the here and now of my reasons – those issues that have been affecting me in the last few months and years. I don't think my early years were a significant factor in my current problems. Maybe I am wrong on that, but for now I will leave most of it alone. The task of identifying the more immediate reasons has been hard enough.

I have tried to focus on the reasons that are ubiquitous, or at least common, for many working people of any age in the 2020s. Work was one of the major reasons for my episode, not only the specifics of my recent jobs, but more generally the overall lack of general fulfilment I find in work.

I am keen to ensure that I don't just focus on a small number of specific areas in my life as being behind my stress and low moods. I want to try and more fully understand the various areas in my life that may have had an effect on my mood.

When I look at many of these areas on their own, they do not seem to be that significant, and most people with a bit of resilience should be able to deal with them. I totally agree with this. That is one of the strange things about mental wellbeing – it's all relative and affects different people in different ways. One person's paranoia could be another's safe place.

The main issue was that I was trying to manage each of these factors at the same time, all of which contributed to my low mood. One or two of these issues at once, or in quick succession, may have resulted in a bad day or a few bad days, but generally I would have coped. The cumulative effect was a significant downturn.

STUCK IN THE MIDDLE SOMEWHERE

Q. "How old are you?"

A. "Ummmmm," (quick memory test), "I'm 47." (Then, in my head, *Really?! 47? How did that happen?*)

I am in my mid-to-late 40s as I write this. Apparently, a classic midlife crisis age. On one hand, that seems obvious and it would be a convenient label. I don't intend to get into the detail of what a midlife crisis is, but it seems that there is a difference between a "midlife crisis" and "midlife stressors" (things that cause stress around the middle of your life). But do the stressors that arise in midlife create the crisis? It seems an obvious link, but, on further analysis, it is, like most things, a bit more complicated.

It seems logical that, as I reach the age that I find myself, the stressors are more numerous.

I am a parent of a young family, a husband, the key wage earner, a son, a sibling, a friend and a colleague.

I have more hobbies as I hold on to old ones and experience new ones.

My work is arguably more complex than ever, and I have more responsibility than ever.

Financially, I am apparently better off than I was many years ago, but I have the burden of a mortgage and other bills continuing for years to come, matched with the reality that my income for the next few years is probably going to be at its current or a reduced level. I am unlikely to get the mega-bucks job or win the lottery.

What I am experiencing now is probably, broadly speaking, my lot in life. It's only now I truly realize that.

Among all of this, I see people making important choices, moving away, getting divorced or taking a fundamental change in direction.

Alongside this, I see people around me getting ill, with some dying.

It seems that at this point in life there are multiple and almost simultaneous stressors affecting those in my age bracket, and they arise from a variety of different sources, both internal and external.

Key to this is that many of these stressors appear to be out of my sphere of influence or control. It feels like I am in the bowling alley and there are people chucking heavy balls at me – all the time.

I have so far concluded that I am resilient enough to cope with one or two negative things in my life, but multiple stressors cause me to struggle. In a way, that is exactly what I believe the midlife crisis is – a simultaneous overload of many stressful influences in life.

This is a simple concept, which I can grasp easily after some consideration and rationalisation. Yet, when I was in the midst of the crisis that included the episode, I either couldn't see it and the stressors, or I could see the stressors, but could not accept that they could not be managed.

Now that I can see this, I feel a little better, a little lighter.

LIFE IS TOO SHORT

In the space of two weeks, I had two friends from one small group who suddenly discovered they had serious heart conditions. The first was one whisker away from keeling over, boom, cardiac arrest, finished; the second was two whiskers away.

The conversations flowed as they each explained their situation to me. The "widow maker" was mentioned – apparently a certain artery around the heart which, if significantly blocked, ends in almost certain death. And, generally, results in a widow.

This was serious stuff.

These were two apparently fit, healthy, energetic contemporaries of mine, with no previous heart concerns. They were basically me in a mirror. As I listened to each of their stories in quick succession, my feelings were strange and mixed.

I was clearly concerned for them, and relieved when they described how the wonders of modern medicine brought them both back from the edge: one had a stent fitted, the other had a full-on electrical box installed in him to do the clever stuff. He showed me the outline of the box under his skin, and the scars and bruises from the recent surgery to prove it.

This was the good bit – the bit which was going to save him and prevent his wife from becoming a widow – but even that didn't look that appealing.

At first, I was concerned, and then relieved. But once the concern for them reduced as it was clear they were going to hang around in this life for a bit longer, it dawned on me… "There but for the grace of God go I."

Before I entered my 40s, I was aware of illness and death, but they didn't really bother me. So why do they have a more profound effect on me now?

The answers are reasonably obvious – I guess I am more sympathetic and empathetic, but the harsh reality is probably as simple as:

- They affect people my age;
- They affect a lot of people my age;
- Which means, will I be next?

We all know that we could be affected by illness at any time. We all live with that; the only certainties in life being death and taxes. But we don't truly believe it. The National Lottery slogan, "It could be you!" rings true, which is why so many of us buy tickets, but do we truly believe we will win the big one? Probably not, but… you never know.

So, if winning the lottery is designed to be on the positive side of "it could be you", then getting some nasty disease or having a heart attack is definitely on the opposite side of the balance sheet. My thoughts tend to oscillate between:

- "I know the chances of being diagnosed with some terrible, debilitating illness which would have a significant negative affect on my life are really small."
- "Well it could happen. Why not?"
- And then, my phone might beep, a message comes in, I am distracted from the concern, and life goes on.

But the niggle of doubt and concern remains somewhere hidden in my brain. So hidden that I don't worry about it constantly, perhaps I don't really worry about it all – or so I think. But then, in the space of just a couple of weeks, I was awakened to the reality of this happening to people who are just like me.

The timing of the news of my two friends' issues was just a few weeks before the episode.

ECONOMIC REALITIES

We all live with our own economic realities, and everyone's are different. In its simplest form, you earn money and you spend money. Sometimes you have a bit of money left, and sometimes you don't. Hopefully, over time the two balance each other out and debt is avoided.

Simple.

My personal circumstances are probably similar to many others. Without going into the detail, we aren't flush with cash, but we aren't poor. We can do much of what we want, but for most activities we have to be aware of what we spend. Pretty much the same for many people, and a lot better than for many others.

If you perceive that you don't have enough money, it can make you feel restricted, that you can't do all the things you want to do or feel you need to do. However, if your financial situation means that you can't even do the things you need to do to stay on an even keel, then you have a problem.

A personal example of this overlaps with an area I cover later: travel, or just simply getting away. This is a pleasure for some, and acts as genuine therapy to many others, including myself. But if your financial situation means that you can't take that much-needed break, then you have a problem.

A number of our contemporaries are significantly better off than us, with total and disposable incomes many times the amount of ours; some probably spend more on holidays than the whole of our disposable income. Yet others spend a lot less than we do out of financial necessity. Many would look at our situation and wonder how we manage to do what we do; we run a small amount of savings, but have limited opportunity to build these up.

I have learnt to live with this, and we kind of get it right. But there are times when the whole long-term reality of our finances takes over my thinking. I think it was such a situation in the weeks before the episode that contributed to my negative feelings. Going around and around in my head was the economic reality that we couldn't do what we wanted to as a family. This is all, of course, completely relative. People would look at us and think, "Wow, they do so much. I wish we could do some of that." Just like I look at others and think exactly the same.

Another hidden and anxiety inducing side of us achieving much with seemingly relatively little is that it is tiring. Always looking for the bargain. Always trying to cut corners. Always aware that if things go over budget, beyond a small contingency, that we won't be able to afford it. I know I bring that on myself – trying to do more with little. But as well as the anxiety it creates it also creates opportunities and experiences that we couldn't dream of if we didn't always look at the way to do it as economically as possible.

When you are deep in that particular hole of over-analysing, you build things into a slightly unrealistic situation. The questions spinning around in my head on an almost daily basis included:

- What if I lose my job? How will we cope?
- What if I just can't go on earning what I earn, would we go under?
- What if our car blows up? The money we have to spend on that will have to be taken away from other things we had planned.
- Without a rise in our income we won't be able to pay the mortgage off until I'm in my late 60s.
- How will we afford to do x, y and z? (X, y and z ranged from "go on holiday" to "fill the boiler with oil".)

Try as I may, I just couldn't look at people higher up the wealth ladder, or even similar to us, without wondering, "How do you do that?" It wasn't jealousy or envy – it was just questioning and more like, "How can you afford *that*?" rather than envy.

I also look at some other apparently more economically fortunate people, whether I know them or not, with other feelings on the opposite side of jealousy or envy. Many people who have so much just seem lost in their own lives and problems, inward looking and blinkered. People who never need to look at a price tag. People who forget or lose something and instead of going without, they just go and buy a replacement item for what they have lost. People who never have to budget.

For some of those it seems that their lives revolve around the purchase of the latest phone or where they will go on holiday next as they effectively strive towards keeping up with those fictitious Joneses. They seem to have everything and dinner party discussions revolve around wanting more, going round and round in increasingly smaller circles of self-desire and consumerism, neglecting what they already have. Many of the same people can act in truly admirable, charitable and philanthropic ways. But equally others seem to have little time for those less fortunate, for helping others or for seeing other's problems.

It's difficult to express such sentiments without appearing sanctimonious or jealous in some way, but I also think as we age and perhaps gain a little bit of wisdom and awareness, one can recognise those more negative financial and human characteristics in others.

Over time, my feelings of stress around money will come and go. They are normally linked to the fact that to sustain our current family lifestyle I have to continue to work in a job I don't really enjoy.

At my lowest times, I think we should just sell what we can, release any equity we might have, and go and live as cheaply as possible somewhere else. To take "the road less travelled," not to drop out but to just get off the treadmill. Simplistically, I see this as a way out, a way of stripping off the straitjacket of mortgage, liabilities and the obligation to continue working in an area which gives me little satisfaction. I would be free!! My mind drifts into thinking what I could do with my time and for work if I didn't have the burden of having to earn a modern "Western" wage − I feel that desire to do something more worthwhile for society in general and more fulfilling for me.

But then reality bites, and with it the realization that pretty much wherever you go you will have bills, and thus need an income. Kids need feeding and clothing, and you will still want to have a few extras and perhaps go on a few trips.

Most humans aspire to more; but when you earn more, you spend more. And one reality of earning more is that generally better paid jobs carry more risk, responsibility, time and stress. So, if one problem was solved by earning more, then new ones get created by the addition of this work stress in life. And other (nicer) problems can also arise as you wonder about how you are going to spend the extra money earned! I am also aware of others in much better financial situations than me who are also far from happy with their lot. A concept which I come back to a bit later – even when you supposedly have everything, you can still suffer from these low points. Stress, low moods, depression know no class, social or economic boundaries.

If I am honest, I think I will always have some financial worries. Or to be more precise I will always worry about finances. At the end of the day, it doesn't matter what other people have or what other people spend, it is what I and my family do and have that is my concern.

Are we spending too much? Maybe. But that is a choice and within my control.

Will we have to work into the future to pay for our lifestyle? Yes, of course. Again, what I actually do for a living and the lifestyle I chose is in my control.

Will we get kicked out of our house for not paying the bills? Probably not because hopefully I can be suitably resilient, adaptable and resourceful in looking after my family.

In essence, and this is what I try to tell myself, we are doing okay. Look at the positives, as you are encouraged to do with cognitive behavioural therapy (CBT); look at what you do have, rather than what you don't have.

At the end of the day, while the amount I earn may have reached its maximum limit, the amount I spend is in my control.

IN MY CONTROL. A key point, which I will return to again. What I spend is up to me. And if I spend less than I earn I should be okay, and

I should be happier. This is not a new concept. As Charles Dickens put it in *David Copperfield*:

> *"Annual income twenty pounds, annual expenditure nineteen six, result happiness.*
> *Annual income twenty pounds, annual expenditure, twenty pound ought and six, result misery."*

So, if this concept is not new and if it's so simple, why do so many of us get it wrong so much of the time?...

I can't help looking at myself and others in a similar situation and come to the obvious conclusion: it is not that we earn too little, it is that we spend too much. Do we genuinely *need* all those things we buy or the experiences we pursue? Probably not. What are the real necessities for us?

It is undoubtedly hard when we live in a world that dangles all these great experiences and products in front of us and which are just the click of a credit card away. When we hear stories of those who have fallen foul of the ubiquity and ease of access to credit, multiplied by the power of advertising, and are in significant debt, we may have some sympathy, but may also think, "Well, you got yourself there."

I take a step back. I am doing okay. It is not the likes of me I should be worried about. I may not have huge pots of money at the end of each month, but I generally have a bit. I should be worried for those who go into debt for the real necessities; those that can't find 50p for the electricity meter, or who have to go to food banks for their family to eat.

And even those problems are relative, thanks to welfare and charitable safety nets. The people who scavenge on rubbish dumps in the under-developed world, those who starve to death and end up on the streets, the refugees who have nothing – their concerns are greater than mere financial worries; their greatest concern is survival.

Nevertheless, knowing there are others far worse off than yourself doesn't mean we stop overly focusing on our own problems or aspiring for more.

Crikey, writing this as I sit in a car waiting for my child to finish their activity which costs money, and which is definitely not a necessity, means I want to kick my own arse.

I have travelled widely, read the papers, watched the news, and I have witnessed and am aware of acute destitution. But still my Western outlook hinders me and prevents me from being truly happy with my lot.

A travel writer once wrote that he keeps a picture on his office wall of an open mine with humans, who look like ants in the vast landscape, working every hour of every day in miserable conditions to just try and feed themselves. To just survive. It reminds him of the harsh reality of life in parts of the world and how relatively lucky we are. I often think of that image to remind myself how lucky I and my family are.

Now, I just have to hold that thought. I started this chapter thinking about how my financial situation means I cannot do many of the things I want to do.

True – still true. But look at all the things I can do!

JUST SIT STILL

"Just relax." "Take time for yourself, to just be, to chill out." Blah, blah, blah. We have all heard it.

"I am relaxed!" I want to shout back. Which kind of sums it up.

I am, on the face of it, a relatively relaxed person. Issues and concerns that seem to send some people off on a whirlwind of worry and anxiety just seem to pass me by.

"You always seem so relaxed and in control," was a frequent summary of how people described me, both before, during and after my few months of low moods. But was it really true?

When I really stopped and assessed how I relax and how I appear to others, I really surprised myself. As I mentioned earlier, I exercise – cycle, run, swim, etc. – I watch TV and I do some gardening. But, on deeper reflection, I realized:

- All my relaxation was "active relaxation" – I was doing things that I enjoyed but they were all active pastimes. I didn't just sit down and relax.
- I would always be doing one activity immediately followed by another. There was very little downtime or transition time.

So, there I was (and still am, but less so), this outwardly relaxed person who did a lot. I was kidding myself that I was truly relaxing. I was good at "doing", but not very good at "not doing."

I also realized that I was probably putting on a face of relaxation – I was acting as if I didn't mind about things, when in reality I did mind. I was kidding myself and hiding my feelings, and doing that can cause stress on its own. More honesty was definitely needed.

This realization hit me quite hard, as I was going to have to rethink some fundamental areas of my life and challenge some of my norms and habits that had been built up over a lifetime. I had to reassess how I relaxed and how I actually acted. Or, to be more precise, I needed to stop acting and be more me, more honest to myself and others. If something bothered me, I should say so.

The thought of doing nothing did not appeal. When I considered all of this further, I asked a few people, "So, what do others do to relax?" I also asked my counsellor, and then followed it up with, "Well, I can't just sit in a dark room and do nothing! Can I?"

The answer from my counsellor to the last question stopped me in my tracks.

"Well, why can't you? Why can't you just sit and do very little or nothing for a while?"

Was *I* talking "Alienese", or was my counsellor?

That definitely had an impact on me. My counsellor was not a Buddhist monk; they were actually much like me. I am sure they used this interaction to shock me into thinking this through more. And it worked. I doubt they genuinely thought I should sit in a darkened room and do nothing; yet, as I engage in meditation more, I realize that is kind of what I am aiming towards, for short periods of time at least. To just "be". To just let the world go by.

My mind, up until now, has almost constantly been very switched on, as if it was a TV flicking between lots of channels and not settling on any one programme. No wonder my mind was tired and overloaded!

I wasn't about to go from one extreme to the next, but there was a realization that, in addition to my "active relaxation", there was definitely more scope for "passive" or "mindful" relaxation.

Could I do both?!

WE'RE NOT HERE RIGHT NOW, PLEASE LEAVE A MESSAGE

One of life's big conflicts, and a source of intergenerational stress for many people, seems to be the physical distances that have developed between families. Although not a modern phenomenon, it is definitely a growing one. For generations, people have migrated and lived abroad, yet it definitely feels like a problem that has escalated over the last few decades.

My family is little different from many others. My parents moved a couple of hundred miles away from their parents and support group. Then my generation went one step further. I have two siblings, both of whom live abroad – one on the other side of the world. And I live an hour's flight or a long ferry trip away from where I grew up and where my parents still live. My wife has one sibling who lives a similar distance, 4-6 hours flying or two days driving away.

There are, of course, advantages. Being able to live like a local when on holiday is a big bonus if you enjoy foreign travel and the mind-widening benefits it brings. We do, and have enjoyed many trips abroad seeing my in-laws and my siblings. If our family didn't live in these places, we wouldn't be able to afford to visit them or to stay for so long.

Individually, you also get to choose to live somewhere that better matches your interests. You also get to make your own way in the world. Not to just end up where you spent your early years but to break away and do your own thing. I, my wife and our siblings have done that – where we live reflects our interests and what we enjoy. If it's urban life you like and your parents liked the countryside, don't worry, just move to a city. Or if you like the mountains but have grown up by the sea – relocate. You get the picture.

But, as we know, for every pro there's a con. So how do the issues associated with distant families manifest themselves?

Well, the problems aren't always immediate. However, as time goes on, and as families grow and people get older, problems can appear. The issues I summarise here are generalisations, but they are pertinent to my recent experiences and to what I have observed in other families' distant relationships.

Grandchildren and grandparents

In the short term, the problems are largely logistical. The multi-generational support network is not there; new parents can't access support from their parents (the new grandparents). Gone are the simple babysitting duties for an hour here and there which were so easy when people lived a few streets away. These could give the parents a much-needed break together, or they could just pop out to run an errand while the grandparents and grandchildren got the pleasure of each other's company. Now the parents need to plan and/or pay for others to be there to help out.

The joys of grandparents spending time with their grandchildren are also curtailed. If grandchildren and grandparents lived near each other, it's likely the relationships between them would be more natural and less pressured thanks to regular, more casual contact; the grandparents can learn their grandchildren's likes and habits and peculiarities – the good and the bad – with less judgement.

When there is significant distance, the same grandparent–grandchild relationship can be more forced and not grow organically. An intergenerational relationship is trickier if it only happens on rare occasions, and then under the microscope of two or three generations being under one roof. The grandparents may not pick up on the grandchildren's nuanced behaviour or not understand what is going on in their young lives, and as a result the relationship can be strained. Likewise the effect goes upward to the older generations as well – the grandchildren don't know their grandparents. Stresses and strains can arise. This in turn affects, often in a negative way, all three generations.

Grandparents and parents

Moving away from your hometown means you miss out on time with your own parents. If you live hours apart, you also don't benefit as much from their wise counsel, emotional and practical support. Modern communication abounds and helps us all — WhatsApp, Facetime, Zoom, whatever — but while this just makes it easier to keep in touch, we still have to put the time in to make those connections.

As people get older, problems arise elsewhere. The care of an elderly relative is a lot easier if they live five minutes away, rather than in another country or on the other side of the world. I am not quite in this situation yet, as my parents live relatively near to my one remaining grandparent and are fortunately in generally good health themselves.

Nevertheless, I realize that as my parents get older, the logistics, the guilt and ultimately the sadness of just simply not being there (or at least near) to care for my own parents as they grow older and more in need will be very present, and will be another challenge for us all to deal with.

All-round family relationships

Inevitably, if friends are physically closer than your own family a different dynamic can arise. The frequent interactions where life's little (or big) challenges are shared over a cup of tea or a meal move away from being with a parent, sibling or close family member, to a friend who lives more locally and who has taken up that position of close confidante. Sure, the family WhatsApp group and regular phone calls have their place, but can such interactions really replace a regular face-to-face chat?

The effects of distance can be apparent in various ways. Firstly, the parent or sibling may be less involved. They can't follow the intricate and daily direction of one's moods or actions; they just have a snapshot and so miss the detail. As such, a regular catch up with a friend can be a more beneficial experience.

Inevitably, over time, distant family members become less involved with your life, which has an impact on the relationship. Does this matter? On the one hand maybe not, but is it not a missed opportunity? I think so.

Hopefully, if we are lucky, the blood-relative relationship void is (partially) filled with a relationship with geographically closer friends, so we can still have the social contact we need as humans. However, while good friends are worth their weight in gold, they more often than not can't replace that unique family bond.

Family is family, and at the end of the day they will always be there. But suddenly interacting and discussing life's matters with them needs more input and time as we are effectively doubling up – giving immediate information of the problem at hand, while trying to fill in the gaps of the days or weeks before. I would love to have had the same discussions about my episode and my low feelings with my close family as I did with my close friends, but the reality is I was talking to my mates who were close at hand and had a greater part in my life.

So, not only did I feel I still had to tell my family, but I knew it would turn inevitably into more of a chore than a pleasure, and unlikely to garner genuine assistance. They worried I wasn't talking, but actually I was, only to others who lived closer.

Good friends who live away

The same is all true for really good friends who live far away.

Just as with families, you can lose touch with friends – even really good friends. Then, when a crisis strikes, you may want to reconnect, but that reconnecting can be exhausting. Instead of that long-term friend having lived through that crisis with you, you now have to reveal the whole story in perhaps one conversation. This an exhausting process, and one that misses out crucial details, which can add to the problem. Certainly, when I needed to talk about my low moods it was very hard to keep those far away appraised, and that in itself worried them. And in turn I missed out on that all important human requirement – to connect with others, to gain a sense of belonging and friendship.

***

But this isn't just relevant to a crisis or to my episode. These distances and subsequent gaps in relationships and friendships can cause real issues in everyday life. And if we don't take care of these little things, then they add up and, "Boom!" you have a big problem… or an episode.

Of course, these are generalizations, but for me they are real. The physical distance between me and many of my loved ones definitely played a part in me not opening up as soon as I could have done about my issues. And then, as I worked through them, I also probably interacted less with my family as well. So, all in all a double whammy on my relationships with these significant others, which, ultimately, we brought on ourselves as we spread ourselves around the globe.

HOME IS WHERE THE HEART IS

On the positive side, where I live has many things going for it. It's a beautiful island. I live a stone's throw from the beach. I can cycle to work. The public services are good. Unemployment is low. It's safe and a nice place to bring up a family. I have friends nearby. The summers can be warm and the evenings long. In short, it's a good place to live.

But every silver lining has a cloud. The flip side is that the place is geographically small, and the population is in the tens of thousands, not millions. The opportunities are good, but in limited areas. The winters can be cold, wet, windy and dark. The culture and pastimes are limited. The variety of opportunities and pastimes that you may find in and around a provincial town or city are not really there. To get away from the place is relatively expensive and needs planning – it is hard to just get away on a whim and, when you do, it requires money for accommodation and travel as you cannot economically take your own "infrastructure" (your bike, your car, camping gear) with you.

In short, I know it is a special place to live, but it can feel claustrophobic and the shortfalls are real. One can feel trapped when it is hard to leave a place – no matter how amazing that place is.

And feeling trapped and unable to get away are big challenges when you may be feeling low, and especially as travel (I like to explore) and time away (even for short periods) is like a tonic for my mind. Travel lifts me up – it gives my mind something else to focus on. So, living in a small place that is difficult and costly to "escape" from can be a real issue.

As with many places, when you are feeling good, then you see the positives and you love where you live. You may bump into people you don't particularly want to see, but that's fine because your mind is in a healthy place. But when you are feeling down, any place can get you down and I think that can be especially true when you are genuinely stuck there. You bump into the same people and you feel no joy; in fact, if you're feeling low there is a desire to actively avoid them. But the smaller the place the harder that is.

But is that the place or is it you? Would you genuinely be happier in a different location? Is the grass really greener? It's overly simplistic to answer "yes" and relocate. You can move, but you may still be the same. You can't escape your mind and your thoughts. And let's face it – nowhere is perfect.

It's a conundrum I grapple with, and I think there is no easy answer. It can be equally correct to stay where you are and sort yourself out, or to choose to move to a new place, or to just take breaks (either short or long) and return with a fresh perspective and attitude.

But being stuck (or feeling stuck) in one place definitely has a negative effect on my mind. I need that break.

HE DIED SUDDENLY LAST NIGHT

The text arrived one Saturday evening. My knees literally buckled and the phone fell from my hand. I was standing in our kitchen and all around me the world stopped and slow motion took over. I read it quickly; it was short but I couldn't take it in.

There was no ambiguity in those five words, yet still I searched for anything that may say it wasn't true. In that moment, the world of my friend ended, the world of his immediate family changed irrevocably forever. In that same moment the world changed for many contemporaries and friends – less so, but it still changed.

"He died suddenly last night."

That was it. That was the text. James had been one of my best friends. The text message was from Laura, James' wife. Suddenly, she was a widow. I still can't get my head round that. James was a few years younger than me and in his early forties.

Shit, it's happened. James was gone.

Grief is something we all encounter and all deal with differently. I am fortunate enough that bereavements have kind of passed me by for many years. When I was much younger, I'd had grandparents die, which was sad and hit me at the time, but the difference was marked – the grandparents were old and I was young. Now things had reversed, I was old(er) and James was young(er).

In addition, when it was my grandparents, I felt one step removed. My parents, uncles and aunts had the immediacy and single line of connection. With James, although I wasn't family, the connection was direct.

It may seem obvious now, but I didn't realize it at the time, that this had a profound effect on me and on my state of mind. James died four weeks before my episode, and his funeral was just two weeks before. I was unprepared for real grief.

I don't want to dwell too much on James' personal circumstances, but suffice to say he had been ill for a while. Despite this, his death was massively unexpected. I had understood that James' long-term illness was likely to be life-limiting, but all the signs were pointing to him having a relatively healthy few years. The life-limiting aspect was years away. Or so we thought.

James died late on a Friday. I had been with him on the Wednesday afternoon – two days before. We had laughed and joked as to how well he looked, even why he was in hospital, and we were discussing the future and making plans.

What added to the impact was my level of involvement in the following days and weeks. A few days before the funeral, Laura asked me to write a tribute to James for the funeral service. I agreed, without question. Crikey, Laura had suddenly lost her husband, the least I could do was write a few words.

I have always believed that if someone asks you to do something for them, you do it, particularly if it's a genuine request in an hour of need. If Laura had asked me to climb on to the roof in a howling gale or walk across a desert then, at that time, I probably would have done as requested.

I agreed to the tribute with one caveat – I would write the tribute but get the vicar, Daniel, to read it out. I felt like it was a cop-out, but I also know my limitations. Laura seemed fine with this approach. We knew each other well and she also knew that I would struggle to read it out. Churches get me emotional at the best of times. I had blubbed my way through my own wedding in a church; I can cry in a church at a good hymn! Add to that, I am not a great public speaker and, as I said, I know my limitations.

I prepared the tribute. I did draft after draft. It was too long. Then it was too short. It was too emotional. Then it was too humorous. I included things that I wanted to say but that weren't really suitable for a tribute. I agonised and I rewrote it. Ali, my wife, as ever, was a massive help. She listened and commented. In the end, I found a compromise and was content, satisfied that it kind of said what I was thinking in my head and that it would be fitting for James, his family and friends.

Once the focus was away from writing the actual words, I gradually realized I had to present it myself at the funeral. I couldn't let Daniel read it. I knew that if I wrote it but didn't deliver it, I would always feel like I had let James, Laura, the family and myself down. I didn't share the fact that I was writing, let alone reading, the tribute with any other friends until two days before.

I practised and I cried. I practised more, and I cried at the start. I practised more, and I cried at the end, and then in the middle. You get the idea. I was not in a state to read it or to say it, yet I knew I had to.

I analysed the crying and where it appeared as I practised reading the tribute. I knew that I would be very emotional at the start and the end. If I could get through the start, then I felt I would be okay in the middle, and then I would be near the end. If I fell apart and cried at the end, then I would just have to deal with it. I would have done what I had to do.

I practised more. I knew I mustn't make eye contact with anyone. I was intent on focusing on the back of the church and over the heads of the congregation. In short, I had a plan and I felt okay. Or I felt as okay as was possible.

In those days, I was dealing with the grief of losing James and it was helpful to have something to focus on in the form of the tribute. But the preparation and thought behind the tribute meant that many hours were spent focusing on him and his death. It was filling my brain. My journey into this grief was deep and it affected me, perhaps more than I realized at the time. There was no distraction from it; I was in it.

During the preparation of the tribute, I went through James's life, our friendship and his family life in some detail. I racked my brains for stories, and articulated them as authentically as I could. It was an immensely difficult and challenging process, which brought his death and all its ramifications for Laura and the family into much greater clarity in my head.

I felt that the tribute bound me closer to Laura, his children and his parents. I felt their and my own pain more deeply as a result of the tribute, as I had been forced to fully confront the reality of this situation.

Unless you are closely and directly involved in a death, I think part of you subconsciously wants to just get on with your own life. I think it's almost an automatic coping mechanism. You know it's happened, and you know they're gone, but it's easy and helpful to just return to as much normality as you can, as quickly as you can. Sure, the funeral is in your mind, and it quickly comes and goes, but then you just get on with life. We all know that life has to go on.

I kept telling myself that my pain and grief was nothing compared to Laura's and to James' children, parents and close family. I knew that. But I then seemed to feel their pain and my own pain more deeply as a result. I put myself in their shoes, which was unbearable. I would wonder how my wife and kids would cope if it had been me who had died. Or, indeed, how I and my kids would cope if it was my wife. Wow, dwelling on it now still pains and upsets me.

Afterwards, as Laura learnt more about the grieving process, she told me that adults become immersed in grief, as if you were in a river; while kids jump in and out of grief, as if they were splashing around in puddles of it. It was something her counsellor told her. I get that. I can't even imagine what being immersed in that river must be like when the loss is of your partner or child at such a young age.

The night before the funeral arrived. We had a long-standing dinner commitment with other friends who did not know James. We didn't say anything about James, the last few weeks or the funeral, and I found it was helpful to talk about other things and to know that the world just carried on. But the knowledge kept reasserting itself – we were burying a good friend in the morning. After they left I then spent until the early hours of the morning practising my words for the next day.

I woke early the next day and gathered my thoughts on a walk alone by the beach. It was going to be a tough day, but more and more I felt sure I had to speak or read the tribute. I knew it would be good all round.

I bumped into another good friend half an hour before the service. He knew about the funeral but hadn't known James, so he wasn't directly connected and wasn't going to the funeral. I told him I was doing a tribute and his face dropped. He turned pale. He couldn't "poker face" this one out. He muttered things like, "I could never do that!", "Are you okay?", "Oh wow, that's something else." Far from helpful. He couldn't help it, he just couldn't hide his feelings.

Crikey, I thought. *If that's the reaction of a sensible, balanced, unconnected person, then I think this is bigger than I'd originally thought.*

Yet I knew I had to go through with it. We arrived at the church. I sought out Daniel, the vicar, who I didn't know and hadn't met; he was brilliant. Laura had obviously told him that he would be reading my tribute, and I told him I had changed my mind and was going to try and read it myself. He looked at me and reassured me it would be fine. We discussed the order of the various tributes and the service. I asked (or perhaps pleaded), "Please, can I go first?" I knew waiting would not be good.

Daniel then said something that was designed to take the pressure off me. "I have never known anyone who has started a tribute, who has not been able to complete it," he said in a reassuring vicarly tone.

My brain processed this. On one hand, that was brilliant! My mind said, "Great, no one has ever not completed it. It'll be fine. I'll be fine. Great news."

No sooner had that particular thought been there and it was replaced, almost inevitably, by, "I am going to be the first one to not be able to complete it! Oh Shit! What if I break?! Will I really be a one-off and act in a distraught, public way that is of no help to James' family and friends."

You can imagine the turmoil inside.

The start of the service was as good as it could be. It was accurate and true to James. Daniel had clearly known James, Laura and his family well, and as a result gave the service that totally authentic, genuine and truthful aspect. It was heart-warming and yet so sad at the same time.

The time arrived for my tribute. I was nervous, but controlled. I had to do the right thing by James and his family. I was determined to get this right for them. But also, if I admit it, for me, for me to be able to do my bit for all of them; this was one of the few things I could do for James, who we had all lost.

I stood up. I walked from halfway down the church to the front. At that moment, it felt like my many, many friends in the congregation looked on with concern, emotion and relief that it wasn't them having to do this.

I could sense it as I walked to the front, and they confirmed it later. No one had known that I had this task ahead of me. I had kept it quiet. I don't know why, but I hadn't been able to tell them. Now they knew, and they saw the stress of grief etched on my face and heard it in my voice as I started.

My preparation seemed to be paying off. My visualisation of this moment and my strategy of looking at the back of the church, over people's heads and avoiding eye contact was running around my head. I knew what I had to do.

My voice croaked at the start, but I kept to my rules. Look at the back of the church and don't make eye contact – not with anyone. But then I had to break my own rule – I mentioned James' children in my eulogy, and one of them piped up, "That was me!" It broke some of the tension in everyone and it really helped. I looked at her, and a tear welled inside as I heard her voice and saw her face, but I kept it together.

Unbeknown to me at that moment, when I looked at James's daughter, my wife's heart missed several beats. She later told me that she was in pieces and in that moment she thought I would also fall apart. But I kept going. The middle part was okay and the end part was, as expected, emotional and I cried. But my part in that sorrowful day was over. I had made it through, and I was deeply relieved.

I watched and listened to the other tributes. These were from professional, competent people. All of them were much more proficient and more used to public speaking than me. Yet in delivering some difficult words they were also emotional. Voices broke, tears were shed and some had to leave early as the emotion was too great.

We were all made keenly aware that the death of someone so young, with a life ahead and young children, was on a different scale to the death of an aged relative. It was a world away.

It was then that I realized that I had done my bit. For James' family. For his friends. But, most importantly, I felt I had been able to do something for him. And I had done something for myself to aid the grieving process.

It was a massive relief that the service was over, and this gave me some short-term strength and peace.

I don't know why I feel it is so important to recount here that experience so vividly. The tribute itself and my part in it was a tiny few square micro millimetres on a giant, wall-sized canvas depicting the vast story of James' life and death and all who were touched and affected by him.

On reflection, I think that his death and my part in his funeral was much tougher on me than I had realized at the time. It was as if the grief had been of a greater intensity and over a shorter period. In some ways, that helped in the long-term, but at the time it had been much harder.

As I said at the start, I had been fortunate to have avoided the full direct effects of grief up to this point in my life. As we get older, I am sure we, for the most part, start to let our own mortality sink in. If you are lucky, when you are young, you just don't have to think about death; it's so far removed from the immediate reality that it's just not there in your mind.

I know many children go through a phase of realizing they and their parents and loved ones will die. But the joy of being young, of living in the moment is so great that we quickly forget about our own and others' mortality. As we get older, the inevitable happens: someone close to us dies. Then – BANG – death is right up in your face and in your mind. This can trigger the reality of our own death and we start dwelling on it.

The grieving process is different for everyone, but time does heal to a degree – life improves, and you get on with it. The river level of grief that Laura spoke about goes down, and maybe you occasionally manage to swim to the shore, get on the riverbank and walk in the sunshine, away from the turmoil of the river of grief that you were immersed in. But you still glimpse the river and you know, one day, you will be back in there when someone else dies. And you also know that your loved ones will be in there, in the rapids, when it's your own time to go. Cheery.

As time passes, I am mostly back on dry land.

As a result of James' death, I was in a more fragile state than I had realized. With hindsight, it is not hard to see that the death of a close friend at a young age had definitely had a deep effect on my mental wellbeing. This significant life event had put me on a downward curve.

And this was just one downward curve of many at that time.

WHAT HAVE YOU DONE THIS TIME?!

Our free time after all the obligations of work, shopping, cooking, eating, picking up the kids, commuting, paying the bills, etc. is, for most of us, so very precious because it is so limited.

How we fill this "spare" time helps to provide us with balance, some pleasure and hopefully joy in life. And if we are lucky enough, or organized enough, then we can use it for activities or hobbies.

For me, physical activity is something that has always been a pleasurable part of my life. I am no elite athlete, but I have always enjoyed a variety of sports: swimming (pool and sea), running, cycling, walking, surfing, sailing, windsurfing and skiing, to name a few. Many of these activities were part of my routine; I felt like I needed them for the break it gave me from reality, as well as for the physical benefits and the interaction and participation with others – that human connection.

Over the weeks and months before the episode I'd had a few injury issues – my back and knee, in particular. They were nothing exceptional, just niggles.

I would recount to friends that I couldn't go running, and they would sigh and ask, "What have you done this time?!" I was known for a few injuries, probably brought on by too many sports, past injuries and not enough warming up or core strengthening.

Without realizing it, I had stopped doing regular sport and was just doing the bare minimum. And, instead of getting the positive benefits of physical exercise, I was struggling with a bad back and other aches and pains. I was feeling frustrated that many of the activities I had previously enjoyed were shut off to me – I tried swimming to help my back and it got better, but then it got worse again; it was very frustrating.

Then, as the usual round of autumn colds took hold, simple, everyday life activities, such as a couple of hours socialising with friends, also disappeared. Relatively quickly, I lost any balance in my life – it went from work playing an important but not dominant role in my life to a life where it felt like all I was doing was going to work, coming home, eating, sitting on the couch, feeling ill and sleeping.

Unsurprisingly, it didn't take long – just a few weeks – for this change in my work/life balance to start impacting on my moods. I now realize that my injuries alongside a series of minor winter illnesses definitely played a part in the development of my negative feelings.

How can I be writing this? Lots of people get a cold and a few aches or injuries, and they are okay! But prolonged injuries and illness, even minor, when weeks and then months go by while feeling bad combined with not being able to do activities which can lift you definitely got me down. It is true that many others feel the same, but again this was just one more downward curve in my life. When it was added to all the other downward curves, the cumulative effect became overwhelming.

NEXT YEAR'S FLIGHT SALE
STARTS THIS SUMMER

I mention elsewhere the variety and number of tasks that many of us take on these days. If we listed the number of different activities we engaged in on a daily or weekly basis, I think it would surprise all of us. It's a useful (if not a little scary) exercise. And if we spent just one minute quickly summarising what our brain has had to cope with over the previous few days it would be immense.

Here are a few from my life: work, commuting, shopping, cooking, eating, dropping the kids somewhere, picking the kids up, telling the kids to make their own way there, paying bills, phoning my Mum, listening to the news, planning holidays, calling a friend, mending the back door, administration, realizing the kids aren't home yet, and so on.

Many activities will be happening to you right now – we are frequently doing, or at least thinking of, several things at once. But, because so many activities need planning, our minds are also involved in considering what future activity we should be doing, with who and when.

We plan. We think ahead. We worry. What we don't do is live for now. Well, I didn't.

On top of all of this thinking and planning is the good old ubiquitous smartphone. Many of the things we do involve consultation with others, and modern communication invariably allows us to consult with a group of people via the smartphone.

The WhatsApp group has replaced the "Reply All" email; it means multiple consultations with multiple people – many of whom have a view on a subject. This constant requirement to consult and discuss to make sure everyone is happy, or at least involved, is often seen as essential – maybe it is – but it's also a real pain, and can block action as much as it facilitates.

I would, at times, think, *Stuff it. I am just going to go ahead and do that on that date.* Then a niggle of doubt would creep in: *But I should just check with so-and-so that they are okay with that.* I would ask them and, it would turn out that so-and-so would prefer to do something the weekend after, thus causing disappointment and more planning as well as unravelling the plans I had already made only to then replace them with new ones.

The desire to do lots of activities requires more forward planning, especially when multiple kids' activities require booking travel and other logistics.

To get the best travel prices when living on an island means booking weeks or months ahead. The constant planning and organization was causing me stress. I would be rolling around in my head the different facets of a weekend that was months away – what flights to take, who to go with, who not to go with, etc. It could be autumn, but I would be thinking of the following summer. Overlaid onto this was the financial worries I mentioned earlier. Could I afford to do these activities? If I managed to bag that cheap flight, book that really cheap accommodation because it's so far ahead, then – yes I could afford it. Just. I really wanted to do whatever it was, so much so that I would make those plans months in advance.

As a result of multiple future events occurring close to each other around the time of the episode, I was faced with many events impacting each other. My brain was making strategic decisions, as if I was playing chess against someone who was much better than me or planning battle manoeuvres on a complex battlefield with multiple enemies. At least, that was what it felt like!

My brain rarely switched off from thinking about some future event. This was overlaid onto similar mental gymnastics required by work projects, whose detailed planning would have more onerous and disastrous results if the plans went wrong.

The result of all that planning was stress! My life was so planned out; I knew what I was doing months ahead. I was keeping myself active, becoming the "busy fool" people talk about. Just people keeping busy for the sake of having something to do, but not focusing on the here and now and not taking the time to work out if what they were actually doing was what they wanted to do or providing personal fulfilment.

Commitment is related to this. Not just commitment for larger aspects of life like a holiday involving flights, but also to smaller commitments like arranging to meet someone. If you commit to something in the future you can then feel trapped into doing it, even though when the time arrives you have changed your mind. Because of this, I would find myself committing to less and less in case I didn't feel like it at the time. As a result, my days were emptier as I didn't have anything to do – because I hadn't committed in the first place!

Related to that is my constant overthinking; the "chimp on my shoulder", constantly nagging at me and doubting me.[2] My brain whirrs away all the time, analysing and reanalysing, going through every conceivable scenario and the pros and cons of each. I overthink and over-plan rather than just letting things pan out or letting nature take its course.

Sometimes this advanced self-organization was great as it meant I had many positive experiences and activities to look forward to. But, negatively, I had little flexibility and I could find myself committed to things that, when the date of the event arrived, I didn't necessarily want to do right then.

What a mess. I was far, far away from the mindfulness of "living in the moment" – I was always partially living in the future.

Again, these challenges could be just seen as "life"; but, without me knowing it, my brain was overloaded with future plans and scenarios and I was really struggling to cope.

---

2   Professor Steve Peters: *The Chimp Paradox*

HERE COMES THE SUN

Seasonal Affective Disorder (SAD) is, as a Google search reveals, a "winter depression, that comes and goes with the seasons. The symptoms seem aligned and similar to more standard depression," such as:

- low mood
- loss of pleasure or interest in everyday activities
- irritability
- feelings of despair.

Treatments for SAD also seem to mirror those for "standard depression", such as lifestyle measures (exercise and sunlight), talking therapies and antidepressant medications.

My episode happened in early winter. I live quite far north in the northern hemisphere. In December there are just over seven hours of daylight compared to 17 hours of darkness! And the opposite numbers happen in the summer – I get nearly 17 hours of daylight in June.

In winter, the weather can be beautifully clear and sunny… and it can also howl with wind, pour with rain and the temperature may barely get above five degrees. And I like to be outside.

The local weather had been unseasonably bad that winter. It was wetter and windier and, as a result, darker than most autumns and winters. As a consequence, the opportunities to get outside and be active had massively reduced.

If you overlay that dreary winter with the knowledge that I get my "buzz" from being outside, then one of the reasons for my low mood is pretty bloody obvious!

Reality check!! Go figure – it's winter and it's likely to affect my mood! I know this, but at the time it can be so hard to really, truly rationalize this. Yet just by typing this out, thinking it through for just a few minutes, I feel better! Eureka!

In a similar way that these seasonal moods can affect anyone, they can also affect people when they are in their "good season". I find that it can happen to me in summer. And then the feelings can, in a way, be more intense, because you think, "This is my good time of year and I am still feeling bad! Oh no! This is even worse."

The pressure can be greater to feel good when the sun is shining because there are (apparently) fewer reasons to feel bad. But I think it is overly simplistic to think, "In winter I will be low, and in summer I will be better."

Winter can be full of amazing, joyful things. The scarcity of the sun can make that rare event of a sunny walk feel even better. There is the joy of sitting inside by a roaring fire, snug and warm with loved ones, when outside the wind is howling and the rain is falling. Roast dinners. Skiing. The list goes on. The Danish call it *hygge*.

Equally, summer can have its downsides. The expectation of a good summer that doesn't deliver can cause low moods. Rain when it should be sunny may be harder to deal with than rain when it is supposed to be raining.

The inevitable tiredness I can feel in summer from being outside all day for weeks on end making the most of the sunshine can sometimes have a negative effect. The neglected "chores" add up (because I am outside doing activities) and cause stress and worry. The inner "chimp" nagging you to make sure you make the most of the summer months can be exhausting.

Simply understanding and accepting that you can feel low at any time of year has certainly helped me.

FIRST-WORLD PROBLEMS

With hindsight, many things that were causing me stress at the time seem so innocuous and simple that I wonder why they ever caused me any worry.

On one hand I look at them and think, "What a moaner!" and "What nice problems to have!" To have many of these choices in my life is a real privilege, and I realize this. But, while I can see that they *were* nice problems to have, the reality is that they were, nevertheless, causing me stress and worry, and therefore they were very real problems. They were *my* problems.

With that in mind, I recall two significant events that were causing me stress during those weeks in the run up to my episode. Our family had two assets that we were trying to sell – a share in a small boat and a run-down second home abroad.

Wow, I've said it! I had assets to sell – lucky me! What the hell am I worrying about?! Why the hell was I stressed? See why I call them first-world problems? And with that admission, I learn a lot.

Firstly, once more I am reminded that to others it may not seem like a concern at all, but if it's a worry to someone then it's still a worry – even if others may think, "Lucky them! What are they worried about?"

Secondly, I am reminded of the fact that if I worry about these things, then the people who I see as having a lot more than me will undoubtedly have their own worries and concerns too. We look at famous or successful people and take great interest in their challenges, whatever they are – debt, divorce, depression, etc.

On the face of it, it's difficult to have a huge amount of sympathy with them as they seem to have everything, especially from a materialistic point of view. But if you analyse their situations further, if they have problems and concerns then they are still suffering. No one is immune to stress; first of all, because we are human; but also, as you achieve more, you have more, and with that comes the expectation that you *should* be happy. We are all in it together, whether you have everything or nothing. We are all prone to life's stresses and strains.

The second house we had available to sell had been purchased many years before – it was a relatively small purchase (in house terms) in a very cheap country in a very cheap area at a time when we had two salaries, more disposable income, no kids and the £ was strong. It had been fun – we'd had holidays there and we'd rented it out. But we now wanted to sell as the money could be much better used elsewhere, if only to try and make a small but psychologically important dent in the mortgage on our house, or to keep some other bills at bay. For years we had tried to sell with no success.

Then an offer arrived. It wasn't great, but it was an offer. And, importantly, it provided us with an exit from a potential liability – a house with a crumbling roof in an earthquake zone could be turned into some cash. Bring it on! But the transaction was a repeating source of concern. The local agent had little idea of how to conclude an international deal, the local tax and legal system were archaic, and the only person driving the deal forward, or so it felt, was me. The exchange rate risk was also real as the economy was going through turbulent times.

The full details are too dull to be of any interest. But finally, after months of emails, chasing, signing and translating many legal documents, the sale finally went through. One source of stress was now out of my life.

The other source of stress was a half share in a small boat, which was also proving relatively hard to sell. I still had the costs and expenses that come with boat ownership while the asset was reducing in value.

The sale was further complicated as my co-owner was in no position to assist – no fault of theirs, and I apportion no blame. All I could see was that I needed and wanted the hassle of boat ownership out of my life and the money in my bank account – again to pay for necessities in other areas of my life. To achieve this, I had to endure the ongoing hassle of chasing emails and keeping the boat in a good enough condition to sell, while getting none of the pleasure that comes from having a boat.

So, what have I learnt through those examples?

That I moan about very nice problems to have! True.

That I had got myself into owning those assets, so I had to get myself out of them. Also true!

That I need something to worry about! Very true.

But the overriding lesson I learnt was that I need to simplify my life. I needed to have fewer of these things to worry about. When I first planned to sell those assets, I was already looking at what I could spend some of the money on to perhaps provide some other pleasure rather than sinking it all into paying for necessities or trying to reduce the mortgage. I did so much research into various options.

But what was I really doing? Searching for something? Trying to relieve boredom or unhappiness or lack of fulfilment in other areas of my life? Probably.

Essentially if I replaced one purchase with another, I was just going from frying pan to fire. Thank goodness I woke up to that before I made another purchase. My life was too complicated; I had made it that way and I needed to resolve it. And one way of doing that was not to go searching for another asset.

I am sure one day I will buy another boat, or something else. But for now, I know I want to simplify my life and not have the burden, the expense and the actual and potential liability of asset ownership hanging over me.

Perhaps I will rent something or perhaps I will just stay at home. Whatever, just so long as it's simpler!

INNER CONFLICTS

I find I have a natural inherent inner conflict; I am happy doing a variety of almost perfectly opposing activities or having opposite thoughts – all at the same time. From one day to the next, I can find joy in one thing which the next day brings me no joy at all.

A couple of examples spring to mind in the context of resolving stress. A key solution to stress can be to do less, to relax more. But then when you stop "doing", you have more time to dwell on things. Then it's suggested that you try to distract yourself from dwelling on negative thoughts, by doing things. At which point I want to yell, "I have been! I've been keeping busy!"

Another example is my need to be near people and to discuss openly my feelings and stress. But I also often prefer to be alone and doing my own thing. "You should do more team sport," I hear myself and others saying to me. But that causes me stress because I can no longer exercise on my own timetable.

Yet another example is in my work. I get bored easily and seek new challenges and change. But that on its own causes me to have more challenges because when places, people and tasks are all new then I have to work harder to achieve what previously may have come more easily.

These inner conflicts pull me in different directions causing even more concern and worry.

JUST LET ME SLEEP

The overwhelming impact of tiredness is not to be underestimated. Any person who feels stress, strain and low moods is normally tired. "I'm so tired." "I can't sleep." "I can't concentrate."

The classic downward spiral of tiredness and low moods – one causing the other to deteriorate, and further down you fall. It is so true, and so hard to break.

Tiredness is a constant backdrop to the times when I have felt low.

The challenge of sleep and combatting tiredness combined with stress is like the chicken and egg dilemma. Which comes first? Often I started to feel tired after I was aware that I wasn't sleeping – obvious. But what was less obvious to me at the time was the impact of stress on my sleep.

At first I would often just put a bad day down to lack of sleep itself, without thinking any more of it. But I soon realized that the lack of sleep was just the symptom with another root cause elsewhere in my life creating this tiredness. Some of those causes for different people are physical reasons, external factors or own goals – going to bed too late, too much alcohol, too much screen time before bed, inactivity during the day or the wrong temperature in the bedroom. There is much written about the basic physical side of getting a good nights sleep.

But I had made great efforts to avoid these own goals or external physical factors. I knew the basics and wherever possible made these relatively simple changes. But I still had a bad night's sleep. My problem was the stressors I had in my life. They were causing my lack of sleep, or rather my waking up and then unable to go back to sleep. My brain would overflow with worries, tasks to complete and the different areas of my life which were out of balance and causing me to worry about them.

Then the vicious circle began. Not enough sleep caused tiredness, irritability and feeling less able to deal with complex tasks, then in time, less able to deal with simple tasks too. Then the stress grew and the sleep deteriorated further.

This cycle was a cause of stress and definitely hard to break.

THE NINE TO FIVE

I knew my job was a contributor to my stress, and one that had to be dealt with.

Just after the episode, I sat down, away from work, and tried to list the areas of my job in which I was involved and/or had responsibility. The page filled in no time. My head hurt just looking at the list as it grew and grew. These weren't little things on the page – these were big jobs that multiple people should be covering, but I was supposed to be doing them all myself!

The observations I make below have been widened to incorporate many of the issues that others tell me about work-based stress from a variety of jobs. This is not just about my job; it is a summary of the elements of working lives that are wrong for so many.

As with many things in life, jobs grow and the to-do list just gets longer. You get on with it while the "powers that be" keep their heads down rather than actively providing support. They think you're doing okay, despite you raising issues with them. But in the main, the day-to-day work, the bare minimum gets done so the bosses are happy; they have other fires to fight.

A key area that I had never really tackled was the lack of personal fulfilment that I was feeling in my job. On reflection, fulfilment is something I have only rarely found in any of my jobs. The sad thing is this is not for want of trying. I have stuck for many years in different jobs and given them a good chance to fulfil me and so that I can perform well and provide an employer with what they are paying me to do. But equally when something is wrong I have analysed it and moved on to do something that is more me – but within certain parameters of needing to earn a certain amount to keep the family afloat.

In many of my roles, I have felt like a square peg in a round hole. I wonder how many people genuinely feel that their job is really using their skills, interests and passions. I know I have rarely found this. It's something that I've thought about over the years from time to time, but the pressures of family life and the need to be the main breadwinner have always put any real thoughts of significant change on the back burner.

So, what are the elements in the workplace of so many that can be so stressful that they impact on life outside of work?

Capacity and capability

Ultimately, if we have the right amount of time, the right skills and tools to get the job done then we're mostly okay. It is almost that simple!

So why the heck do so many people and so many businesses get it so wrong?

There are competing needs from many people – clients, colleagues, investors – as well as family life and your own needs. You need to have enough hours in the day to do your work *and* engage in life beyond work.

And even if we and/or our team have the capacity to do our work, we may not have the capability – the experience or the training, for example.

Attitude

Now this is an area that still troubles me, and I go full circle on it. Is my attitude wrong, or is my attitude absolutely right? As ever, it's complex. Different people have different attitudes – they may not be right or wrong, just different.

One can care and be diligent. I care that the job is done well. "Caring too much" is likely to be seen as a positive attribute, but it can often lead to negative feelings and consequences. People "catastrophize" – their minds run away with themselves, thinking the worst will happen. Of course, if you are not given sufficient resources (capacity or capability) to do a job then the worst can happen!

Equally, you need to be pragmatic and proportionate. Life isn't perfect, and work isn't either. In most jobs there is a margin of error, a tolerance, and the end result will be the same regardless. For example, a pilot doesn't put the aircraft down on the centre line of the runway every time, but he still lands the aircraft successfully.

You get the idea. There are acceptable margins for error and tolerances. Agreed, if the pilot slams the aircraft down in the wrong direction on the wrong runway, then we have a problem. But almost everywhere there are tolerances. And success can still be achieved without being 100 per cent right.

So, it's fine to care, but it's also important to know when we can have some slack.

Responsibility

People have responsibilities at every level. But as you move up the career ladder, responsibility and accountability increase proportionally, and these can weigh heavy. It is vital that responsibility and accountability are fully understood by all.

In their working lives people need to have the freedom to control what they can, and they should not be hassled about areas that they can't control. If a project, budget or target is not in your immediate control, you shouldn't be reporting on it and you shouldn't be judged against it. I have seen many occasions where people are penalised for something that they had no control over. Such managerial practices can cause huge stress to the individual concerned.

Investment

Work can be summarised in three key areas:

- People
- Systems/tools
- Processes.

Each of these areas needs frequent and significant care and investment. In many industries and sectors, investment can be very hard to come by and can be lacking for years. As a result:

- **People** are underpaid; people are under-skilled because they haven't engaged with up-to-date training; and there simply aren't enough people to do what is required – the capacity point has been reached.
- **Systems** (IT especially) are old and unreliable, or simply do not work.
- **Processes** are not fit for purpose but lack of capacity means there is never the time to ask, "Why do we do that?", so people carry on doing what they did before – creating ongoing inefficiency.

Management and decision making

There are some fine managers. And there are some terrible ones.

Early on in my career, I was managed in a global organization by a guy who later became one of the top executives. He was very impressive. The key criteria to his impressiveness included:

- He always made you feel like he had time to spare to talk to you.
- If he ever asked for anything, he had a three-step process:

  o Used first names directly and clearly – we all knew who was going to have to do what.
  o A short but clear instruction – there was no grey area of what was trying to be achieved.
  o A "please and thank you" in discussion – his politeness meant you wanted to work for him.

Importantly, he had great judgement, and as a result whatever he asked you to do was part of your role, within your capability and for a valid reason – and, as such, you bought into it.

Clearly there is so much more to management than this, but it is a very good start. So, why do many managers get it so wrong and seem to neglect the basics I mention above?

Security

If people feel safe and secure they tend to work better. If people are constantly worried that they will be moved on, or their job will be reviewed and radically changed, then they tend to spend time thinking about that, talking about it and looking elsewhere – all to the detriment of actually doing the current job!

Flexibility

Flexibility is a two-way street. The employer and the employee need to be flexible for the relationship to work, but more often than not, the employee has to be much more flexible than the employer. The employee is at the beck and call of the employer with things like overtime and extra duties. And when some flexibility in return is requested and denied, it is a one-way route for the employee–employer relationship to ultimately fail.

Planning and implementation

A common problem in larger organizations is the imposition of ideas, projects and initiatives without due consideration. Poor project planning and implementation is rife in many organizations.

The individuals left responsible for implementing the project then don't believe in it and/or don't fully understand it, resulting in the project being implemented badly, inconsistently or not at all.

Or sometimes changes that are not needed are implemented anyway. Always ask: is it change for good reason or change for change's sake? If it doesn't pass this test, then forget it – just don't bother.

As well as poorly implemented initiatives, there can be just too many. Sure, we all understand the need for change. But when too many new changes and projects are implemented at once they are often all done badly and/or they take too long. Initiative overload.

Appreciation

Most people want to feel appreciated – to get that warm feeling of genuine appreciation. Sure, most people get paid, and for some that is thanks enough. To work for years or months without acknowledgement is very poor. Many organizations seem bad at showing thanks beyond the financial reward.

Finally

Work can be complex.

Work can be richly rewarding or deeply frustrating.

Work is just a part of life – do the work to the best of your ability, professionally and take pride. Then go home.

A final word on jobs in general and how I perceive the problem where people are not being fulfilled is changing – for the better. The advent of technology has shut many avenues as more process orientated jobs are automated. However, the variety of jobs seems to be growing all the time. Technology has opened up many more opportunities. Creativity and celebration of difference is now encouraged and proven to be more fulfilling, and a plethora of jobs has opened up.

A skilled career adviser (with the use of technology and bespoke tests for the person they are advising) can suggest so many more different types of jobs for this up and coming generation compared to 20-30 years ago, when the previous generation completed their education.

Gone are the days when only the stereotypical jobs were on offer – the unfair classing and stereotypes of "skilled" and "unskilled" or "professional" and "non-professional" which has labelled so many individuals across the generations and created a barrier for those who want to change. So many people just fell into the job they are doing, rather than being allowed the freedom to make a choice. Part of this was just lack of choice, true.

But there is so much more. The current generation also seem to be encouraged to dream and to "think big." Whereas previous generations were told to "get a job."

Another part was the expectation that, in the past, once you had been labelled as one thing you just fell into a particular career. Good enough for university – get an office job, move up the corporate ladder; left school at 16 – you can't be a "professional"; get a trade. Generalizations, yes, but true. I feel that I have definitely been one of those who just fell into a traditional career route without being allowed the freedom, time and space to really think, *What do I want to do as a career?*

In the solutions chapters I analyse how we can all be aware of and tap into these different and new careers and jobs. Current and future generations will benefit from much of this automatically but for those who have been working for many years in unfulfilled careers, the challenge is to break out of the traditional stereotypes wherever possible. It is hard and the need to earn a certain amount is still a huge challenge and barrier. But at least we can try.

PART THREE
POTENTIAL SOLUTIONS

SOLUTIONS TO MY STRESS AND LOW MOODS

The old saying goes something along the lines of, the hardest part of solving any problem is admitting or understanding there is a problem in the first place.

When I was feeling low, I did have a problem understanding that there was a problem at first. Then after the episode, I was pretty damn sure there was a problem, but it was difficult to find solutions at that point because I felt so rubbish.

So, it is all well and good understanding there is a problem, but I had a greater challenge to try and work out any solutions that would hopefully help with my issues. But I had to make a start.

"Sustainability" is an important, but often overused, word today, but it was perfectly appropriate for the types of solutions I needed to put in place. They couldn't be quick fixes to solve an immediate problem as this enables it to reoccur. Soon after the episode, I started to understand that I had to make some significant and sustainable changes. An easy win was to reduce work stress by taking a break from work – but this was not a long-term sustainable solution.

It was good that I could reduce one problem with a simple short-term solution, but I was keen to find sustainable and longer-term solutions. I knew that just hiding from or avoiding stress was not a reasonable or sustainable solution!

Can many of my other "challenges" be truly solved or eliminated? I doubt it. Nevertheless, it is key to work towards this goal and be positive enough to really believe that a significant amount of the issues can be massively reduced and some solved. I definitely believe that can be the case.

At first, I was just keen to come up with a bit of structure and some simple solutions to treat the symptoms that I was feeling so acutely. In time, I hoped I would be able to come up with solutions and actions to treat the root causes as well.

There seems to be a huge number of different solutions out there to stress and low moods. Many of these will be familiar to us: rest, relaxation, perspective, exercise, maintaining balance, meditation, connecting with friends and others – and I make no apology for the fact that there are limited truly original ideas in my list of solutions.

I see familiarity with most of these solutions or strategies as a massive positive – if much of this is not completely new to me, then surely the solutions will be easier to master, and I can become happier more quickly. That thought alone is a relief. However, it is one thing to have heard of a solution and quite another to truly master its skills, understand the detail and have the self-discipline to build the practice into our every day lives.

It is also the case that many of the solutions are new ways of doing things we already do. I, like many others, have fallen into habits – many are bad habits that do not engender a healthy mind.

One simple concept is that negative thoughts breed more negative thoughts – it's a downward spiral. We feel low, we overthink things, and then the fact that we are worried about worrying fuels and deepens more worries!

So, although the overall concepts may be familiar, I am having to learn new ways of doing old things. I am having to break bad habits and try and develop new ones that are better for my mind. This, inevitably, takes time.

I am no expert in these areas, and there are individuals and experts who are much better versed in explaining and practising the various solutions. What I can attempt to do is give a layman's description of some of these solutions and how they worked for me. Some of these solutions are helping me now, and I know that if I don't reflect on them and capture them now, I am liable to forget and fall into old, bad habits.

I have tried to split the solutions into two main categories.

- General principles, or ways of thinking, which I can hopefully try and use much of the time to help in all areas of my stress and low moods. These are less specific actions and more ways of living.

- Specific solutions, or actual activities, to focus on – not necessarily every day, but just to make sure I include these things in my life in some way. These can be easier to achieve than the general principles because I can just say, "Right. I am going to do 'x' action for ten minutes." The key is making the time to do these activities… and to do them effectively.

An important "health warning" or caution about my solutions is that:

- these have worked for me at this time, but may not work for me again in the future or for others; and
- when you use multiple solutions you can never truly know whether it was an individual solution or a combination of the solutions that was most effective. It's a bit like taking more than one medicine for an ailment – which medicine actually worked? Or would I have recovered anyway, even if I hadn't taken the medicine? Or if you have a bad back and the physiotherapist gives you numerous exercises and stretches to assist your recovery – which one really made the difference? And which were unnecessary? As you can't be certain which were the "money" or "killer" exercises – the ones that really solved the problem – you may have to keep doing all of these exercises even when some are not actually helping at all.

IT'S GOOD TO TALK

A big part of my healing process was discussing my situation with others.

At first this was challenging. I was still working out what had and was still happening – to some extent I still am and will be for a long time. I struggled with describing the situation accurately. I was also in the midst of feeling low, so although I knew talking about it was a positive thing, it was also really hard to do. It's not the easiest topic to discuss, and not everyone wants to hear about it.

But I was keen to resolve the issues, and knew talking was a necessity, so I went for it. At first, it was hard to identify who was interested or who had the time, the listening skills or the empathy to want to listen.

Once I did talk, the reaction I received from the many and varied people who I opened up to, was truly incredible.

Over the past few years there has been a general opening up about mental health and the need to discuss it, particularly in the media. We have heard a vast number of people, from senior British royals through to radio DJs, singers, YouTubers and television presenters, talking about their mental health journeys. Although it could be considered trite to recognise their input, what they and others have done, I believe, has been really crucial in allowing others to open up and discuss these life matters. I certainly took their lead, and it has been as powerful as it has been eye-opening.

In so many of the conversations I have had about my woes, it has led to the other person opening up about either their own similar experience or that of a partner, colleague or friend. You name it and, almost without exception, they or someone close is feeling it too.

So why have I not noticed this as much in the past? I think you only truly open your eyes to something when you really feel it and have direct experience. I, like many, generally have greater sympathy than empathy skills – "Walk a mile in another man's shoes", and all that.

I have learnt over the years to listen, and I normally feel more comfortable asking questions rather than divulging personal information to others. These characteristics, combined with being able to keep secrets and confidences, have meant that many people have opened up to me about personal issues in the past, but not half as many as have now opened up to me about stress, anxiety, low moods and anything in between.

The fact that I was not alone was comforting, and it also confirmed my initial hunch that many, many people were dealing with similar problems and challenges. This reignited my desire to try and understand the whole problem and possible solutions – not just for me, but for others. My original desire for starting this book was to help me understand what had happened to me and how I could help myself. But in time I was determined to complete this book in the hope that it could help others who had been through similar experiences.

While people may open up to talk about their physical health, many people still don't feel comfortable talking about their negative feelings, their challenges and, to put it clumsily, their mental health (the term alone can have negative connotations and stigma attached).

But if you go first and tell other people your story, and you choose the right environment, person and time, then the dam gates open.

Whoooooosssshhhh.

The stories flood out. People with similar and related challenges to me are literally everywhere. I clearly cannot and would not break any confidences here, but I have been massively surprised, shocked and heartened by what I have heard.

I am fortunate enough to mix with people from many demographics. I know manual labourers and tradesmen, board directors of large companies, professionals and partners of global firms. A few examples of the stories I heard, both directly and indirectly, from my diverse group of contacts spring to mind, such as:

- Government officials who have taken months off work due to stress, with some having to stop working altogether.
- Successful entrepreneurs who have anxiety so acute that they can't function in anything but their specific business, and who have to "disappear" or "go off grid" for lengthy periods while they "reset".
- Teachers who, after decades of work, have resigned from top positions to take time off and then return to an entry-level job.
- Senior executives who wake in the middle of the night unable to sleep as business cash flow projections, or some other worry, go around and around their heads.
- Chief Executives who have just walked out of the office door one day and never returned.
- Ordinary, admired people, who many consider to be chilled and relaxed, having anxieties, insecurities and/or vicious tempers.
- Married friends opening up about marital difficulties and depression.
- Truly inspirational, successful and elite individuals who lead a double life of outwardly being fine and true to their image but within are wracked with anxiety and self doubt.

The "unloading" of much of this suffering on me (and my wife, through me!) was first and foremost a blessing, but I have to be honest that at times it was also a bit of a curse.

We ended up with an acute awareness of the pain and mental suffering that many, many people were going through. My wife and I used to talk about how we felt as if we had "absorbed" some of these negative feelings and so genuinely felt for and empathised with those who were close to us.

It was hard, really hard. But I had to remember that their pain was not our pain – there was no way we could take on all of their problems and challenges as well as our own. Sure, we had a role to play as confidantes or listeners, but we had to make sure it didn't take my wife or me down further. We could listen, question, sympathise, empathise and help, but we had to gain some perspective and focus on ourselves as well.

While there are connections between these people and their stories, equally it seems that anyone can be affected – the rich, the poor, the young and the old – stress and anxiety is indiscriminate. Having said that, I think the problems do seem to disproportionately affect people in their 40s, and slightly more men than women (although because they are my contemporaries, my sampling size was skewed towards this group).

But whatever the statistical bias, the reality is crystal clear to me. Anyone who suffers in some way is most definitely not alone. And talking about your feelings is a massive part of the recovery.

As well as talking to people I knew, I found it helpful to talk to people who are trained in listening to and helping people with stressful situations. When you add into the mix a decent therapist who has the skills, tools, experience, framework and objectivity to assist you, then you get real value. I often used to (only half-jokingly) say that we should all have a permanent therapist. Again, I realize it works for some and not others; but, for me, I have so much running through my head that it is really healthy to talk through life's challenges.

The limited times I have seen a therapist or counsellor, after specific traumatic experiences, have always been worthwhile; maybe not life-changing or a solution on its own, but definitely worthwhile. Each session has made me look at things slightly differently, and I have had several moments of clarity where I have realized something that has previously been hidden from me.

Out of all the possible solutions, talking, to anyone and particularly to a professional, seems like a no-brainer. It does take time (and money when a professional is involved) but it is definitely worth the investment.

There is another side of this talking which I should mention to ensure balance and reality is maintained. The assistance I mention from talking to those around me was real and very helpful. However, it is also worth mentioning that not every encounter was successful and not everyone has the skills or sympathy to be of assistance.

I mention this to make sure that if people who are suffering from low periods try to engage emotionally with someone else that they should not feel disheartened if not every discussion provides them with solace. I was also surprised by how some close and long-standing friends seemed, on the face of it, indifferent, unable or unwilling to take the time to be interested in my obvious plight. In my darkest times I took some of this personally and I translated this into real disappointment that they did not care or I unfairly thought of them as emotionally inert.

The reasons why some people fitted into this category are complex and most people did, I am sure, still care in their own way. Some may have been going through their own challenges. Others were no doubt just very busy and caught up in their own lives. Others are not as comfortable talking about emotions. For some the timing was just wrong. And for some, they just live on a very even emotional keel and just have less to add.

But in the main when I did talk to others about my challenges and feelings I was impressed with how most people responded. Most of these conversation provided great comfort at this difficult time.

REST AND FRESH AIR

Okay, let's start with the mind-numbingly obvious but which most of us rarely achieve. Shortly after my episode, a close friend just texted me four words of advice: "Fresh air and rest."

Originally, I wanted to add "and exercise" to this, but now I think that exercise (or the type of exercise I do – running, etc.) is separate to this. Too much exercise can impact your rest (although some exercise can aid rest as you tend to rest better once you have been outside and done something!).

Rest and fresh air were really important to me in the first few weeks after the episode. I knew I wasn't getting enough of either as it was all too easy to stick with my old habits of trying to fit in lots and not take care of myself. I was shattered – from what had happened with the stress and low moods and from what I was trying to do to solve the problems. My body needed a rest.

Just doing less was part of my recovery. It was hard, but crucial.

I read about the power of power naps and I tried to take more of them – just taking the time out helped.

Then there was the fresh air. I used to get this from running and cycling. Both are great, but they can also result in *too* much exercise. The good old walk was rediscovered. Wow, it had some benefits – I would feel better just from taking a walk round the block or being in nature. It didn't even have to be a very long walk to be effective. Then, as I walked more, I realized different types of walks had different value to me.

Occasionally I would walk alone and try and avoid people. These were generally taken when I wanted to gather my thoughts – to think without interruption or to use the silence to try and mull over a problem. I tried not to dwell on negativity during these lone walks, as I realized there was a risk with this. Sometimes I would walk listening to music through headphones, which helped distract me from my own thoughts. I mixed the lonely walks up with other types of walks, and it really helped.

I would walk with others for company and for a chat, and use it to catch up on the day's events.

I would walk in rain or wind or sun, again for different reasons. The rainy/windy walks would give me that idea that I could "take on the world" despite adversity. Let's put this into perspective – it was hardly going to the South Pole, but the winter weather or length of walk could still create challenges. The sunny walks were there to remind me that the rain, the grey, the clouds would shift and there was indeed blue sky still out there. I used that to remind me that my mood would also shift and I would overcome my darker moments.

I would do long hikes for hours or short walks of just a few minutes. They all had their value. This chapter is centred on rest and fresh air, and as a result an inevitable focus on the shorter walks was important during the early stages.

I have read whole books on mindful walking, and I don't intend to even scratch the surface here on the therapy a good walk can provide. However, it is probably one of the single most significant and beneficial activities that I have found in my recovery.

I mostly used to try and leave my phone and watch at home when I walked, which reduced the inevitable distraction. If I did have the phone, and I felt like it, I would make some notes as to how I was feeling and of the thoughts that would arise on the walks. I recently found some of these notes on my phone, which, to me, sum up some of the benefits of walking.

Overleaf are the notes from a lone walk, many weeks after the episode, on a sunny day, after many days of rain. It seems to sum up and witness my awakening to being more in the moment and the realisation that I would get better. My mood was loosely correlated with the weather. I think it was more than just a coincidence that thanks to the sun, my mood was also starting to lift after a while of feeling low.

It was a good moment in what otherwise may have been a bleak day. In part, thanks to a simple walk.

Today I can hear and feel the crunch of the ground under my feet as I walk.

I feel the wind and see it moving my hair and my clothes.

I can feel the beat of my heart and my lungs expand as I breathe.

I hear the individual waves crashing on the beach and see the sparkle in the sea under the sun.

I can look up and see the blue sky and the sun beating down after days of cloud.

I can once again feel that I am almost living in the moment rather than in the thoughts and worries whirling around my head.

I don't know if this is mindfulness or just a good walk, but I can definitely start to believe that, as people have told me so many times, "Soon it will pass." Whatever "it" is!

Until now I have not been able to believe that.

JUST RELAX

As I've already explained, my mind is almost constantly switched on. And not just in a normal "on" mode – if I were an electric bike, I would be in "turbo" mode rather than plodding along in "eco" mode. If I were a car, I am in sixth gear bombing down the motorway, not tootling along a country road with a nice stop at the pub. No wonder my mind was tired and overloaded!

Outwardly, I was quite a relaxed person, and felt the same inwardly. I felt I enjoyed relaxing activities and was able to chill like others. But in reality, I rarely truly "reeellllaaaax" enough to engender a truly relaxed body and mind.

So, what are sustainable solutions to achieve more relaxation?

Take a deep breath

Meditation and mindfulness have definitely helped me. As I do more meditation, I realize the value of having a calm, quiet and relaxed mind.

While I still can't have a quiet and calm mind for long periods, I am able to achieve a *calmer* mind for some shorter periods. This is a massive step in the right direction. At least my brain, as well as my body, can start to have some down time.

In my head, the idea of guided meditation had some hippy, new age vibe or connotation to it, but, ironically, thanks to the "app for everything" world we live in, I found it was easy to access many positive programmes. The app I use has made guided meditation immediately and easily accessible – all I need to do is ten minutes in a quiet place, and I can manage this.

The basic premise is that, through the app, someone calmly talks you through what to do and you just listen and follow it. I am no expert, but it assists me with breathing techniques, calming my mind, and assessing and understanding my mood and feelings. The best thing about it is, at its basic level, it is very simple to follow.

I am sure some people will benefit more than others from meditation, but if a frequent or, better still, a daily habit can be formed, then meditation has massive benefits. For this beginner, who finds it hard to switch off, these ten minutes of calm give my mind and body a partial rest from the almost constant doing and thinking.

As I got more into it, I realized that I needed to be able to both practise it without the app (unguided) and use the meditative skills during my daily activities. This has been harder than the ten minutes a day, but as I get slightly better at the basic skills and really start to feel the benefits, then I find myself making more effort to do this.

And come on – ten minutes a day?! Surely that's possible. Then, in time, the ten minutes can turn into more of a way of living. The meditation won't be restricted to those ten minutes a day. Your brain will adopt a new way of approaching life, helping you to be in a more mindful state throughout the day. The ten-minute slots will then just help keep you grounded, or topped up in that way of thinking. Meditation in this simple form has been a huge help.

I now actively seek a quieter mind and am more open to doing less rushing around and just taking a bit of downtime at different points each day. It can be a challenge to sustain this, but even just adopting a few small changes helps.

Meditation and mindfulness are clearly linked, and I am a mere novice in each. I see the minutes of meditation like filling the car with petrol, and then I try to be more mindful throughout the day as I drive the car (my brain) around. I try to be more mindful and aware of what I am doing most of the time, and I am aware that I can only drive the car in that way because I stopped to fill it with petrol (that is, I stopped for a few minutes to sit and meditate).

If I find myself being less mindful, or more stressed, and less "in the moment", I have picked up a few practices that can help bring me back to the moment and put things into perspective:

- Leaving a coloured Post-it note on my desk at work. It doesn't say anything on it, but is a reminder to be more mindful, to be more present in this moment. If I see the coloured note, it jolts me back to the moment.
- Pausing, shutting my eyes and taking several deep, long breaths. "In through the nose, out through the mouth." We've all heard it, but I try to do it, to remind me to be in the moment.
- Taking a short stroll round the block – alone – just to look around, breathe some air and have a different view.
- Doing a five-minute admin job, such as checking a bank statement or paying a bill, to help me feel more in control.
- Really focussing on the task in hand. Whether it is typing on my computer or being in a meeting, I try and really focus on that task; I listen to the clicking of the keyboard as I type, or try to block out all other senses and focus 100 per cent on what the other person is saying in the meeting. With this level of focus, time can run away with me as I am "in the flow" and the task at hand just takes over. This practice may not last long but it can jolt me out of a negative moment.
- Pausing, shutting my eyes and doing a quick body scan, I try to feel every part of me, from head to toe, to reconnect with my body in order to feel good in that specific moment, even if it's for less than a minute.

These are small and simple things. They are not quite second nature to me yet, so I have to remind myself to do them. And sometimes they don't work, but with more practice they seem to become more effective.

Before the episode, I would not have done any of these things. I was probably not even aware of the benefit of such simple actions to keep me here in the moment appreciating the things around me.

More "unproductive" time

Another solution for me is to be more open to doing seemingly unproductive things. Before, if someone asked if I wanted a cup of tea or to take a few minutes' break from whatever activity I was engaged in, I would invariably politely decline and just carry on with whatever I was doing. I would see that break as unproductive or unnecessary. I am now more open to those short but important moments of downtime or additional social interaction with people who I come into contact with.

Not stopping for a quick cup of tea or a brief chat seems ridiculous now. But I can genuinely say that I was not open to those situations much in the past. At risk of huge generalisations and appalling gender stereotypes, I think that women have a far better approach to this than men. Women are often more open to taking the time for a little chat or a coffee.

Those social interactions and the catching up with another person have multiple benefits. And a bit of time out with someone else can be a relaxing as well as a productive, connecting and engaging experience. Time spent with others has other benefits as well – it enables conversation and shared experiences, and provides the opportunity to talk things through. It can be a very healthy pastime, for mind and body. Essential for our human spirit and being.

I have definitely opened up to this and try to do it more, as I understand its value for both myself and others. In the past I may have seen it as non-productive and a waste of time. Slowly, I am learning.

Old habits die hard

I like watching TV; I get a lot out of it and I find it relaxing. But I am aware that when I am feeling a little low and tired or it is dark outside, I can all too easily resort to my old habit of watching *too* much TV, especially in the winter when there may be less to do.

A certain amount of quality TV and a certain amount of "mindless" entertainment is fine. In the past I would watch quality programmes alongside a fair amount of "because it's on and because I can't be bothered to go and do something else!" But I have tried to change my approach to TV.

Firstly, I try and watch less. This has multiple benefits as it allows me more time for something else, such as listening to music, calling a friend or just catching up on admin (which, if I allow it to build up, causes stress).

Secondly, I try and only watch things I am genuinely interested in and which I enjoy.

Thirdly, I try to turn it off well before I go to bed. That creates more time to do other activities more conducive to preparing me for sleep – reading or talking! Not exactly mind blowing or original activities, but better than inane TV!

Now let's be clear here, I am not about to give TV up for good as it still gives me pleasure, but I now enjoy better-quality TV at times that benefits me in other ways.

Leave more time

Instead of leaving exactly the right amount of time to get somewhere, I try to leave a few minutes earlier. This reduces stress if the journey takes longer than expected, and if I arrive before time, then I have a few minutes to just sit and be.

This is a simple practice that is really helpful.

EXERCISE IS THE KEY

For me, the benefits of a walk, which I have already mentioned, are different to the benefits I get from exercise. A walk is more passive for me, or at least less active than the cycling, running, etc. that I class as exercise.

The benefits of exercise are significant and, as we know, well proven. The endorphins released lift the mood and physical feelings. I hear more people talk about serotonin – the "happy chemical" that contributes to wellbeing and happiness – and guess how you get it? Yep, through exercise (as well as other ways, including diet).

Many people seem to be addicted to exercise, and it is definitely something that needs to be built into my life and my sustainable solutions.

I think I kid myself that I exercise a lot.

I cycle on a daily basis to work, but that is more a mode of transport (to avoid traffic and the need for parking spaces and to guarantee a short journey time) than exercise. Sure, I get some exercise from it and it helps a bit, but I need to do more to feel the benefits. I cycle "the long way home" from work to get some extra benefit, and will also go for an hour-long cycle on occasion.

I swim regularly and it helps, but in a pool I find that less fulfilling and a means to an end rather than an enjoyable activity. In summer, I swim in the sea, which I prefer.

I surf (occasionally) and that can have the multiple benefits of physical activity, a challenge, exhilaration and mastering a skill, as well as talking with other like-minded people and being surrounded by nature and slightly scared by waves and the swell.

I run (when I am not injured), and that can give a quick buzz.

On a less regular basis, I paddleboard, windsurf, sail and ski. I live far from the mountains, but when we do go it is significantly beneficial. All those physical activities have the double benefit of being exercise and out in nature. I have never been one for exercising in the gym and I now realize that, subconsciously, it was only doing half the job for me. Sure it was providing exercise but it was missing those benefits from being out in nature and out in the elements while I exercised.

As I get older I play less competitive sport or team sports and in a similar way to sport in nature, competitive and team sports can have multiple benefits of exercise, competition, challenge and human connection. Again, I need to seek out more of these opportunities now I have appreciated their value on multiple levels.

Another, almost daily, activity I do is the YouTube workout. It's easy to skip this, but, wow, does the right one work? A positive side effect of the first coronavirus lockdown in 2020 was the emergence of plentiful daily workout videos on YouTube. No equipment was needed, just get yourself into the lounge and get on with it. It lacks the natural element but as a winter activity which is quickly achieved it was and still is a huge help. One of my favourite coaches even calls himself "Captain Serotonin!".

I also stretch and exercise, but this is more a by-product of managing my ageing body and trying to minimise back and muscle pain. It also means I may avoid injury or general aches so that I hopefully continue to do even basic exercise and just get through daily life without some kind of pain or ailment. I am not going to kid myself that 15 to 20 minutes of stretching to keep my bad back at bay is yoga. My kids are *Star Wars* fans, and at the time of my low feelings, all they could talk about was Baby Yoda. This was also when I was doing more of my juvenile, even baby, attempts at stretching, and "Baby Yoga" soon became interchangeable with "Baby Yoda".

When I look at this list, I sound like a pretentious sportaholic! But the reality is very different and it doesn't feel like that to me. When I analyse it more deeply, I know I benefit so much from exercise and I really enjoy each of the activities.

OXYGEN MASK ETIQUETTE

Yet again, I am about to attempt to try and summarise the completely bloody obvious – the importance of making sure you have time for yourself. But if it is that obvious, why do I and (I am sure) many, many others not practice it as much as they should?

One phrase that really drove home to me the importance of self-care was, "Always fit your own oxygen mask before helping others." This safety instruction is issued on flights, and the message is clear: if you aren't in a good state yourself then you will not be capable of helping others.

There are times in your life when you have to put yourself first.

A few years ago, when my kids were pre-school age, I was loving being a dad and being fully involved in their lives and activities. But, frankly, I (like my wife!) was knackered. Burnt out and neglecting ourselves, we were focusing massively on our kids to the detriment of ourselves. It was classic behaviour for a parent of a young family with a busy job. I was chatting with a good friend (who had older kids) when we bumped into another friend who had become a dad a couple of days before. My friend with the older kids gave one simple line of advice to the new dad, "Make sure you take time for yourself – now and over the years." I literally stopped in my tracks. *Crikey*, I thought, *Why the hell didn't he tell me that a few years ago?!*

I definitely had a blind spot. I was super-focused on my kids (and enjoying it), but I was definitely neglecting myself. I had given up many activities and the kids were the priority.

I am not advocating going from one extreme to the other – neglected children is not the way forward. I see contemporaries and friends who work too hard. Children who are starved of parent time seem to be a root cause of many family challenges and problems as the kids get older. What is needed is more balance, and this certainly applied to me.

I needed more time for me to do the things I enjoy – my hobbies, my activities; my wife needed more time for herself; and we needed more time for and with each other.

I think the practices of the current parenting generation is a contributing factor in this. I was catching up with an old friend recently as we were assisting with our kids' weekend activities and she joked, "When I grew up, my parents just made sure I had clothes and food. They left the rest to me!"

I know this was exaggeration for effect, but compare the weekend of a kid 35 years ago to the myriad activities that kids do and which involve parental input (if only to drop them off) – it's bound to have an impact on parents' free time and wellbeing.

Now, I don't want to go back to the "old days", and I think kids now benefit from many of the extra activities in a way that my generation did not, but I do think we need more balance.

In the months running up to the episode, and in the years before, I had definitely neglected time for me. I am still torn between wanting to spend time doing things for myself and doing things with my kids. I take them to school, I watch their sports games, I drive them around, I read with them, etc., but I also realize that I don't need to do these things *every* day and to the detriment of me doing activities for myself.

I think turning this knowledge into practice is a key solution for me. But it is also one of the hardest to implement. There won't be a sea change in me, but I hope to push the pendulum slightly the other way.

Another reason for not going too far the other way is that doing more for others is actually good for you. Altruism is good for those you help and it seems to be proven that it also helps the person putting the time in – that person gets a kick out of their good deed.

So, another solution is to do more for other people. It's a classic "conflict" position – you need to do more for yourself *and* more for others. Do more! Hang on, I thought I was supposed to do less? Again, balance and moderation seems to be the key.

I am reminded of a sign on a friend's wall: "Happy kids. Tired Parents." It was designed to be one of those inspirational mantras and to sum up a happy family life. But does it have to be this way? I know kids are tiring and parents get tired, but as adults we need to make sure that we have time for ourselves. I guess we owe it to ourselves, our families and our kids to ensure that we take care of ourselves first. Because if we don't fit the oxygen mask on ourselves, we are definitely not going to be in a position to help someone else put their mask on and support them through life's rollercoaster.

MORE HONESTY

We all worry. Humans seem to worry about anything and everything. It just seems to be different things that we worry about. A realization and acceptance of this knowledge that humans are prone to worry is a deep part of helping me deal with worries. The fact that I can now be more honest with my feeling is also a big help.

Related to this is the difference between the real person and their online profiles. When I look at a specific person, I see each person as they simply appear on the face of it – just their outer physical self and the way they interact – and most people look fine and pretty okay with their lot in life. It's only when you take the time to interact and get to know someone that you start to understand their true self.

When people put their profile online then the focus is on just a specific aspect(s) of a person – the aspect(s) they choose to show. We all know that people aren't all beautiful and on holiday all the time – they aren't always having fun, which if we only focus on some people's online profiles or stories, we may be lead to believe.

The real person is going to work, getting stuck in traffic, arguing with the kids and feeling stressed and anxious about certain things. When I remember this, I don't feel so negative, different or low. But when you are feeling low, it's easy to forget reality when you see the rest of the world apparently looking happy and smiling on Facebook, Instagram, YouTube videos or whatever.

We are all in this together!

I also came to realize that, just like those images of others' perfect lives, maybe *I* wasn't being honest, but in a different way. Perhaps I wasn't being honest with myself as to my true feelings.

As I have already mentioned, I realize now that I don't truly relax. Nevertheless, people saw me as a relaxed person, when inside I now know I wasn't, and even though I think I am reasonably honest, it is easy to just show the "game face." It was easier to just go along with others preconceived ideas of who I was or how they saw me.

Most days we are faced with the same question: "Hello – how are you?"

"Hi. I'm fine, thanks." We all give the same reply, but inside we may not be fine at all.

Now, let's be honest here, honesty can be as dangerous and risky as it can be powerful. We have to counter our desire to be honest with the reality of living a normal life. When the bus driver says, "Morning, how are you today?", we can't really spill the full reality of our feelings!

If we all truly spoke our minds then we'd soon get ourselves into trouble. But honesty that is measured, carefully considered and well-meaning usually works out best in the long term.

I think a bit more honesty from me when I am stressed is a very powerful and helpful tool as it avoids keeping too much locked inside. Before the episode, people around me just didn't know how I was feeling.

But I have to be careful to not use others like sponges that can absorb negativity! We all know those people who just unload on you without a thought for your own feelings. We also all know that inspiring, "radiator" people (who radiate warmth and positivity) are definitely more fun!

I think that I need to get the balance right and be more honest. As I mentioned earlier, my honest discussions (at the right time!) with so many different people, reaped huge rewards for me and for other people who were then able to open up to me about themselves and their own challenges – each discussion helped both parties. If I hadn't been honest about how I was feeling, none of that would have happened and neither party would have benefitted.

SEEING RED AND UNDERSTANDING WHAT IS IN MY CONTROL

We have all done it – sat there, in the car, happily driving up to traffic lights that are green and then, just as we approach, the lights turn red and we have to stop.

Now, to me, how we react to this is a great way of telling us what kind of mental state we may be in. Not necessarily the long-term mental state but also the feeling on that day. Granted, it makes a difference as to whether the light goes red when we are late, or if we are going somewhere important, or who is in the car with us. And I guess that is exactly the point! More of that later.

The reaction to this red light is generally somewhere between these two extreme states:

- Person A: "You fxxking lights, why is it always me? Why do they turn red just when I am driving up to them? Fxxckin fxxckers." The driver then sits there looking at their watch, gently fuming as the other cars go through the corresponding green light. They impatiently rev their engine ready for the lights to go green and then speed off.
- Person B: They don't even consider the lights to have gone red suddenly. They don't see anything individual to them. The driver just accepts that when the lights are red they have to stop their car, they wait patiently until the lights are green and then off they go.

So, a few key personal questions for me:

- Am I Person A or Person B?
- Which person was I in the run up to and just after my episode?

- Which person do I want to be in the future? And not just with traffic lights, but in every tiny obstacle or challenge that arises.

A bit of further context before answering the above questions.

- What if these lights were the tenth lights in a row that had gone red on me?
- What if I was running late for a really important meeting?
- What if I'd had an argument with the kids that morning and I was feeling irritable already?
- What if I was totally lost, the satnav was broken and I was in a city I didn't know?

If the answer to one of those context questions was "yes", then I may be more likely to react in a way similar to Person A.

What if every single context question was a resounding "yes" on that morning? Well, let's face it, "Person A" was definitely present!

Around the time of my episode, I was in a vulnerable position and the context around me was very negative. So, when an obstacle arrived (my metaphorical traffic lights) I was liable to react badly. I was definitely more the "fxxxing fucxxer" Person A type than serene Person B.

No great surprise.

But there are many obstacles that are completely beyond my control, and it is important to remind myself of that: they are out of my control. And because they are out of my control, reacting like Person A just exacerbates the problem. So, all I need to do is to identify what obstacles are beyond my control and then not worry about them. I try to do this.

I try to ask myself a simple question:

"Is this totally beyond my control?"

If it is, then I should just forget it. Ignore it. Be more like serene Person B.

You may even be able to use the time you're waiting at the traffic lights wisely – look at the environment, notice something specific and focus on it, do your pelvic floor exercises! I don't care! Anything. It doesn't matter. Or maybe just do nothing. Empty your brain. Just sit there. Whatever you choose to do with this extra spare time, it will almost certainly be better than being irate for those few seconds (most likely) or minutes (at most).

Clearly, there are often grey areas. Is this obstacle really beyond my control? What if I do have some control over it? These grey areas are harder to deal with. But whether I do have control or not, the skill and the solution is to just try and treat things in a similar way. A line from Rudyard Kipling's poem "If" springs to mind:

> *If you can meet with triumph and disaster*
> *And treat those two imposters just the same.*

But let's face it, the odd red traffic light is not a disaster!

DON'T FIGHT FIRE

Time is one of our most precious commodities, and one most people wish they had more of.

So how we spend our time, how we prioritize all the things we need/ want to get done in the day, the week or the month is going to have a big impact on how stressed or calm we feel.

Much has been written on this subject, and there are various management gurus who have researched and philosophised on this over the years. One such writer was Stephen Covey, who is a bit of a legend in management circles. Rarely does a management course go by without Covey getting a mention. He is to management a bit like what Colonel Sanders is to fried chicken or what Captain Birds Eye is to fish fingers. You get the idea.

Well, Covey, among his multitude of great discoveries and clear articulation of the blindingly obvious, had a theory on time management: try to "spend your time" rather than "manage your time". Covey also used a Time Management Matrix – a good old quadrant – basically, it's just a box split into quarters of urgent and not urgent, important and not important.

Apparently, the key is to spend more of your time on the important but less urgent topics. That way you will, overall, be more likely to reduce the amount of important and urgent topics. You have achieved the task before it comes urgent. You should be less stressed because these things aren't urgent (yet!), but as they are important to you then you get fulfilment, both immediately from the act of "doing", as well as later when that completed important thing is providing you benefit and has not turned into a stress. I understand most of this and, after review, have added some suggestions in the boxes.

Sure, you will have to spend some time carrying out urgent tasks – answering the phone, paying bills that arrive late, etc – but don't spend *all* your time in this urgent or "firefighting" quarter – spend more time on the important stuff, which isn't yet urgent.

Tasks - Time Management Matrix (from Covey) - with some additions

- Spend time in top left quadrant. BUT also:
- Work out where your strengths lie
  - Do you thrive on pressure and stress? If so, work in top right Or
  - Do you prefer to plan and work diligently and carefully? Work in top left.

Important	Spend most time here +ive - have time to perform the most important tasks to the highest standards -ive - not every important task can be planned	Firefighting / High pressure work +ive - can drive good performance; forces action -ive - can cause stress, especially if always spend time here
Not Important	Try and eliminate - Why are you even looking here - These tasks are not important and not urgent - Forget them or delegate	Spend minimal time here Delegate if you can (if they really need doing) - Arguably these tasks aren't really important, so why are they urgent? - Inevitably there are tasks which we may not see as important but eventually they need doing
	Not Urgent	**Urgent**

Tasks - New / old activities (hobby, job, sport) in a familiar / unfamiliar environment (place or person).

The key is to spend some time in all four quadrants. Achieve balance. But accept and understand that there are advantages and disadvantages of each.

New Activity (e.g. hobby)	Friendly familiar environment to try something new +ive - safe place to make mistakes, try new things -ive - will you really progress, be free to genuinely innovate if it's too safe	Risky / Exciting +ive - learn new skills, develop, can have freedom to make mistakes -ives - can be stressful, out of your depth
Old Activity (e.g. hobby)	Comfort zone +ive - can perform well; something you enjoy -ive - boring	Chance to do familiar activities with new people, in a new place +ive - pushes your boundaries -ive - not necessarily easily available
	Familiar Environment (e.g. place, person)	**Unfamiliar**

ROUTINE IS (NOT) THE ENEMY

Many, many years ago I took a few weeks off work between jobs for some time out. It was great, and the reasons for needing that time had some similarities to what I had experienced before my episode – although I only realize that now. When I told one of my less traditional contemporaries that I was taking a work break, he smiled in a "good for you" kind of way, and said, "Great idea. Routine is the enemy."

At the time, I thought, "Yeah – look at me, doing a bunk, bucking the system, escaping the routine. Nice job!"

And I still think there is some virtue in escaping the routine. Yet routine can also be important, and it proved particularly so for me in the early weeks of recovery after the episode.

In those early weeks during which I was off work, I felt dreadful, and knew I was very lucky and privileged to have this time away from my usual work routine. However, I soon realized that some routine was a vital part of my recovery and, as I got better, I liked having some routine. Apparently, this is very normal.

Just as children need routine to feel safe and secure, so do we as adults. Perhaps we have just been so ground down by certain routines that we need a different or new routine now and again. The key is finding a routine you like! And also feeling that you have had some input into the elements of the routine.

In those early weeks I tried to do too much, before I found the right flow – first of all, doing less, then adding in some routine. It's amazing how you can go from juggling everything (or trying to) to a much simpler routine that still fulfils you.

My basic routine in the immediate few weeks following the episode was pretty simple:

Morning: Wake. Spend time with family. Breakfast with family. Help get family out of the door. Cycle with one child to school. Take a long cycle home. Think/write/read. Stretch. Meditate.

Lunch

Afternoon: Rest. Read. Listen to the radio. Meditate. Walk. See kids after school.

Tea

Evening: Kids to bed. Read. Meditate. Talk. Small amount of TV. Read.

Sleep (or try to).

Ok, it wasn't exactly Buddhist monk level of calm, but equally it was nothing like my old routine, or that of a normal working dad. It was simple, very unstressful, the same every day, and that's what I needed. It definitely helped.

I know I was incredibly lucky to have the opportunity to live that simply. Even just realizing the benefit of this simple routine was really helpful to me.

I can now see that when I returned to the working world, where a routine is inevitable, that I need to keep some control of the routine, and make sure to leave time for the things that are of value to me. I also know now that routine can be beneficial whereas before, in the midst of my stress, I saw routine as an enemy, as an imposter and as a cause of my stress.

It's all too easy to get stuck in a rut or routine that may not be healthy. It's easy to just continue with old activities, old habits and old ways of thinking. I think the whole process of understanding what has happened to me has illustrated this.

In addition to trying to build solutions to stress and low feelings into my life, I think I could form a way of assessing and looking at new and different things to do. Too many new things all at once can create stress, plus my usual activities and ways of thinking are not all bad. So, perhaps a similar matrix to that applied to time management by Stephen Covey could be used to create a good combination of new and old, familiar and unfamiliar.

I can see that different things could be put in the quadrant, such as:

- Activities
- Hobbies
- People
- Places
- Holidays

I may not want everything new – new faces and new places – all at once. But perhaps I could introduce some new hobbies in some familiar places, or vice versa, to freshen things up and do things a little differently.

I have realized that I need a balance of my old favourite activities with some new, different things. To mix it up. To keep it real. To keep balance and perspective.

GO WITH THE FLOW

It may not surprise you to know that as I have already touched upon, I have a tendency to overcomplicate things. I over analyse; I play scenarios out in my head. I forward plan; I visualise the reality of scenarios. I strategise in my head; I like to think things through. I also like to do things properly – properly as I see it, that is.

These traits can have massive advantages. It means that I can normally predict how I will feel in a specific situation, and I can then avoid situations that I know aren't really for me. At work, I can pre-empt some issues, plan accordingly and take early avoidable actions. Some of that comes from experience but a lot comes from planning and thinking things through in some detail.

As a family, we don't make too many "bad calls". You hear of other families who have whole days that are just, if everyone is honest, a bit shit, because they haven't planned. For example, not realizing how long it would take to get somewhere, so the family sits in a car for hours on a day out only to find the place they are going to is about to close. Or, the family who is shivering on the beach in a strong onshore breeze with cold kids and sand blowing in their faces, while 15 minutes away there is a beach facing the other direction basking in heat and everyone is having a great time. Small things, but not inconsequential. There can also be more major, life-changing problems from a lack of planning. For example, thousands of pounds wasted on a holiday abroad in the wrong season.

So, as a result of my aptitude for planning, I can foresee some issues and find techniques and solutions to overcome them. So, on the whole, this has put me in good stead. We generally have good experiences and avoid many bad ones. But OMG, can it be dull and frustrating for me and others!

I can be like the wise (dull) old senior work colleague or uncle in the corner who has seen it all before and warns of doom round the corner. It also means that by the time I get to my perfect beach at the optimum time I am exhausted by the amount of strategising I have done to get there.

I need to lighten up and go with the flow a bit more. I think there is more scope for me to throw everything up in the air and see where it lands now and again.

So, next time you see some family who have driven for hours and arrive just as the attraction that you're just leaving after a good day out is closing, have a thought for them, because:

- they don't have everything planned to the last degree; and
- the person responsible may be (the "new") me!

DO I REALLY NEED THAT?

My generation's tendency is to own things. Or to at least try to. People's garages are full of "stuff" – multiple bikes, BBQs, gardening tools. We have also grown up with a disposable attitude to many of our assets – something breaks, buy a new one – rather than the old way of repairing things. And owning stuff can be time consuming, expensive and stressful. There's the initial cost and then the responsibility of maintaining things, and maybe guilt if you don't fully utilise your purchases.

So, all I need to do is to buy less stuff! Is that it?

I am definitely getting better at this, but we all know the story: if you have a small cupboard, you fill it. And when you have a big garage you just fill that too.

I am making an effort to acquire less. Or if I do buy something it's because I really need it and will use it for a long period of time. Not just because I think I need it. It's the old, "Do you want that or do you need it?"

This solution may become more meaningful with the next generation; how they will "consume" major things, such as houses and cars, is looking like it may be different to our generation's pre-programmed desire to "buy and own".

The next generation, partly due to constraints on their finances and time, as well as better technology enabling short- and long-term rentals, seem much better at consuming what they want when they want it. They don't own, they rent – both big and small things. For example, they use Airbnb accommodation rather than aspiring to own a holiday home; they car share; they use Boris bikes in major cities.

I am fortunate to have been able to buy various things (or I was when we had more money with both my wife and I working without big family financial commitments). I am definitely going to consider renting more in the future. And, before that, I will take a long cold look at the item in question and ask, "Do I really need that?" If the answer is an unequivocal "Yes," then I will look to rent.

Clearly, there are some things that just make economic sense to own if you can, like your principal property. But there are many other items that can be rented with less stress and hassle, particularly if only required for a short time.

It is the less stress and less hassle features that I am keen to pursue. And hopefully the garage door will be able to open all the way as well.

MINDSETS TO LIVE BY

Through all my thinking and analysing I've realized there are a number of "mindsets" or "ways of thinking" that are almost the backdrop or context to how I should try to think, act and live.

Acceptance

Accept the inevitable and focus on the things that are important to you.

The first few weeks after the episode were a little bit like putting my life under a microscope.

Things I have always done and thought were positive elements in my life were suddenly not helping. One of these things was my desire to "just get things done". I had my lists and I ploughed through them. I suddenly had time on my hands so thought I could do all these things that I "needed" to do. I got worse – my mood got lower.

I soon realized this was the wrong approach. All this "doing" was not healthy. Much of this book has worked that out.

Also important was accepting that I can't do everything. My to do list will never be completely ticked off so I can sit in the sunshine with no jobs to do. There will always be something else.

I have always known that I can't do everything I *want* to do; I also now know that I can't do all the things that I *need* to do.

I also now know that lots of the things I think I *need* to do actually aren't that important anyway. I don't *need* to do many of them at all, or if I do need to do them, I don't need to do them *now*.

I mentioned earlier the process of learning to focus on the "important but not urgent" matters and I found this to be helpful. Categorizing life's activities and needs in the right boxes – either important (verging on genuine need) or not important – is, for me, well… important.

Beyond accepting that I can't do everything on my ridiculously long and complex lists I compile, I am also trying to learn to live with the undone things around me. For example, should I care that a specific room in the house still needs decorating? No! It will never be perfect! Sure, I can do some decorating so it doesn't look like a squat, but I don't need a show home!

This extends to accepting which things are in my power to change and which aren't. The key is recognising the difference between the things I can't do and those that I can do or can change.

This idea of acceptance is nothing new, as best expressed in Reinhold Niebuhr's "Serenity Prayer":

> *God, grant me the Serenity*
> *To accept the things I cannot change,*
> *Courage to change the things I can,*
> *And Wisdom to know the difference.*

Wow, those guys knew a thing or two, back in the day.

Appreciation

Smell that coffee – no don't just think about smelling it – actually smell it!

Appreciation should be frequent, mindful and of the small things.

I need to remind myself to do this – to really take the time to appreciate my life.

I need to remind myself about the wonderful, often small things that truly make me happy. As I run from one task to the next, I need to take stock and be grateful.

> *Enjoy the little things in life, for one day you may look back and realize they were the big things.*

Robert Brault

This period in my life has demonstrated to me how many people have been there for me as I have gone through my struggles. I have massively appreciated and been genuinely humbled by the number of messages, enquiries, words of support, reading suggestions, little gifts and other things I have received. People have gone out of their way to seek me out and be helpful.

In particular, there are a handful of people who have really been there and thoughtfully assisted me, despite, or perhaps because of, their own busy and challenging lives. The assistance from many has been so great it's almost been too much. I can only have a certain number of conversations, a certain number of chats in cafes or read a certain number of books that have been recommended to me. I really appreciate every single one of my friends and family who has provided that support.

That alone has taught me that friends and family are the important things. I do now appreciate them more.

Don't operate at capacity

Leave some headroom, with enough time and money to be flexible.

I have probably over analysed our own family's "limitations" in life – time and money. I have also discovered that many of the things I thought to be limiting factors probably aren't limitations in reality. The limitation is in my mind. I can do a lot. I realize that.

Inevitably, human nature nudges you to wanting a bit more and then you forget the amazing things you can do if you are just happier with what you have and make some good choices and prioritize appropriately.

So, when I hear a voice in my head or a feeling inside that says, "You want (or need) a little more," then I need to ensure I have built some flexibility into my life so that I can do those extra things. For this, I need to ensure that there is some money and time available. It may not even need to be very much of either. This is important, because when I feel I can't do something because I am nearing capacity it can create stress for me and make me feel trapped.

The solution is to keep something in reserve – time, money, energy. That way I should still have options. I just need to not over analyse those options, and instead get on with doing the things that are genuinely important to myself and my family.

Reading the signs

Balanced optimism as a way of mind and as a barometer.

I really need to approach things with genuinely balanced optimism.

I need to believe in the most positive outcome, but also do some minor planning for a different outcome.

When I do this and when I don't is usually linked to my frame of mind at the time. When I am a bit low, I end up being pessimistic, and when I am feeling better, I am more optimistic – it's only natural.

I now see that I can potentially use this self-awareness as a kind of barometer to measure my mood. If I know I am being overly pessimistic, perhaps it is a sign that I am about to feel a bit low or may be low already. I should take that knowledge and use it to trigger some of the other solutions. I should also consider why I am feeling low – perhaps I have been neglecting some of my coping strategies, or I've been ill, or not taken enough exercise, or not been outside enough or not been meditating.

Commitment

Flexible but thoughtful, well communicated and fair.

Commitment generally has caused me some stress. I am often conflicted between wanting to commit to things but to also retain some flexibility so that I don't feel trapped or obliged to do something that I've changed my mind about by the time it comes around.

As a result, I can end up not committing to things and being left out of life's pleasures with family and friends.

If I say I am going to do something, then 99.9 per cent of the time I do it. If I have given my word, I find it very difficult to break it. My innate sense of duty means that once I have committed to something, I must go through with it, as I don't like letting anyone down.

I wonder if there is a way to be "flexibly committed", without turning into an unreliable, verging on selfish, person who lets people down at the last minute – the kind of people who are responsible for the ever increasing (and frustrating) "cancel culture."

I'm learning that you can commit to certain things, but in the right situation you can have a 'get out'. If that obligation really isn't the right thing for you to be doing at that time and any other party is treated fairly and told up front about the reasons for the change, then I think it may be okay to let people down gently now and again. It's okay to let someone down gently for a good reason.

If there is a genuine reason for a change in plan, then I think most people are understanding. And surely that has to be better than me turning up to things out of duty, getting little joy out of it and so not really contributing anyway. Present in body, but not in mind. "Presenteeism" in HR speak – you're there, but you may as well not be! That causes me stress and achieves little for me or the other party.

THE VALUE OF A BREAK

Taking a break from routine and everyday life has long been acknowledged as beneficial. From when spa and coastal holiday towns started accommodating short stays for the affluent, people have benefitted from breaks. The increasing popularity of holidays can perhaps be attributed to the growth of the middle class.

The concept of a break is similar now to 200 years ago, but I can see that there have been some key changes, which include:

- More people can now access a break – the original "grand tour" of Europe in the 18th century was only available to those of sufficient rank and wealth – it didn't extend to the masses in the way that EasyJet et al now enables.
- The duration of a break has been extended – it's no longer just a Sunday break from the working week. It's often not even just a week's holiday either – there are now long weekends, fortnights in the sun, gap years and sabbaticals, to name just a few.
- The frequency of breaks has increased. An annual holiday may, for the lucky few, now be just one of several trips taken in a year.
- The locations available to us for a break are multiple and can be far away; for many more people, the world may not exactly be their oyster, but it is definitely more of a possibility for more people.

At this stage, I should caveat this with the reality check that I know that many such trips are not available to everyone. I know that the hard graft and economic realities of the lives of many mean they stay at home for a lot of the time. However, I also know that many others do go away, whether it be for a long weekend staying with family and friends, or for a year-long sabbatical involving the whole family and multiple foreign countries.

The characteristic each trip, from the short to the long, from the staycation to the global ramble, has in common is that the traveller hopes to gain something from it that they can't get at home. Otherwise, why go?

A break from the everyday, no matter how short it is, can be amazing. "Travel broadens the mind." It's an old saying, but true; entire books have been devoted to the life-altering effects of travel. There is the "push" factor encouraging you to leave home and get a break from the norm. And the "pull" factor of what you will see, experience, do and enjoy when you arrive at your chosen destination.

Sure, modern travel and crowds and airports have their downsides. Go to most "on the map" tourist destinations at the height of the season and the wonder can be short lived. Bournemouth beach on August bank holiday Monday? Not much peace. Venice in August? No thanks. Popular French ski resorts in February half term? Come armed with some patience and remortgage before if you want lunch. London museums between Christmas and New Year? Get there very early and be prepared to join the scrum. You get the picture!

But parking those aggravations and disadvantages aside, the value of a break (if chosen wisely) can be immense. A break is definitely a solution of kinds, but not on its own, or in isolation.

Many of the problems you're taking a break from will be waiting for you after the holiday has ended. I understand that condition, but I am still first in the queue to get away whenever I can. This is because the "right" break: to the right place, with the right people, for the right length of time and for the right reasons, should sustain us to face those challenges we face on return in a different and perhaps better way.

The part I am struggling with as I deal with my difficult past few months is what kind of a break do I really need? Part of me thinks we should carry on enjoying breaks away, but overwhelmingly we need to enjoy being at home more and appreciate the great things and people around us.

The best things in life are free, and ultimately we are often happiest when we return to our roots, familiarity and home. Where we feel connected and a sense of belonging with people and place. But the question I am grappling with is "Do I *need* to go on an adventure?"

I have itchy feet. From an early age, I have always wondered what is over the hill or round the corner. I love to see new places and experience new things. How much of this is escapism from a life not totally fulfilled, I am not sure. But even when life is good, I always love travelling and feel a need to visit new places and meet new people. Living on a small island also feeds a need to "get off" it at times.

Many people get itchy feet, but the realities of life cement them to the spot: the kids are too young, you don't have the money, what about work, etc.

Around 20 years ago, I was lucky enough to head off for a few years, and I worked and travelled in distant lands with my (now) wife. The experience had highs and lows. We had some memorable experiences we could never have had during a lifetime at home. We connected with people and places we would never normally get to meet or see. We had a fresh outlook and become more open-minded, resilient and understanding of other things and other people. We also appreciated more about our own home country and environment.

Importantly, the feelings and positivity of that time have remained with me for a long time. In the 20 years since, when other people have headed off to far-flung lands, I was lucky and fortunate enough to know what many of those places were like, that I was lucky to live where I lived and, as a result, I felt fairly contented.

Two decades on and perhaps I need another "fix". A bit like a car needs a service at various intervals to get through the next period of life, perhaps I need another boost. Perhaps I, as an individual (plus family!), need a longer break to enjoy and sample what is out there, remind me of what is important and to sustain me into the future.

But so many questions abound.

- Where do we go?
- How do we afford it?
- Is it really achievable or just a pipe dream?
- What will the kids do?
- How would we school the kids?

- Should we work? What would we do?
- Should we just travel?
- What will we miss out on at home?
- Should I just knuckle down and get on with "normal" life?
- Am I just running away?
- Should I sort out all the problems here first before I go away? But will that mean I never go away?
- If my (working) life was more sorted here would I feel the need to go away?
- What about our ageing parents and those around/near us?
- What about the kids' connection with their friends?
- Are the kids the right age?
- Am I just doing this for me, rather than for the good of the whole family?

I just don't know the answers. What I do know is that I find it hard to ignore the more fundamental questions behind this underlying feeling of restlessness without going somewhere else.

My conclusion for me and my family now? Still undecided, but deep down I know I will make every effort to go.

On balance, I will stay at home and resolve some of my issues here first – to try and put in place many of the solutions, and strategies. And then head off to… who knows?

I need to accept that I (and we) will never get everything resolved. There will always be something to deal with, including satisfactorily answering the questions listed above; gaining an understanding of my "challenges" and how we resolve them – which basically means finishing this book and tying up loose ends here – from the big (deal with the house, sell the car, minimize our life here) to the small (cancel Netflix, and the myriad of other jobs).

We also need to ensure that we have something really good to return to – a solid foundation from which to build again, so that we won't starve and so that our return will be a pleasure. If we were to fear returning, it may force us to stay away longer and for the wrong reasons, and it would also probably taint some of the pleasure of being away.

So, I think we should plan to go somewhere for a significant period of time (not years, but also not weeks or months) to somewhere and to do something that will sustain us. And maybe we will stay away for longer.

If so, great. If not, then hopefully we return because, to us, home is preferable, which is surely a good outcome!

Overall, I know that we will "throw the balls in the air" and then see where they land. Throw caution to the wind and just do it. Just get going. There will always be a hundred reasons not to do it. Going is definitely harder than staying.

But in life, what you put in is what you get out.

NUTRITION

"We are what we eat."

"Eat well."

These phrases are so obvious, they hardly seem worth a mention. We all know the benefits of eating well, and that what we put in our bodies as fuel is definitely going to have some impact on how we feel. But it can be tough to pull off.

Suffice to say, I am no exception. I try to be healthy where I can. I would say we, as a family, generally eat healthily, but with some room for improvement. I am not obsessive, but I have tried to cut out chocolate, sweets, biscuits, crisps, etc. This makes some difference, but probably not as much as I think.

One major factor in my wellbeing that I realized soon after the episode was the negative effect of alcohol. I never really felt the depressive side of alcohol before, but as I mentioned earlier now I know it can get me down. If I know I am in a difficult period, I now go teetotal. The only sadness in this is that I enjoy a social drink. It seems a shame to be denied the odd beer or two with friends. But fortunately I also now know that when I am doing fine then a healthy amount of alcohol can have significant benefits − both mentally and physically (as the benefits of a small amount of alcohol on a regular basis in later life now seems to be proven).

In the first few months after the episode, I eliminated alcohol almost completely. However, recently I have been able to enjoy alcohol again − not in huge amounts as I am wary of the negative effects, but I can have the pleasure of the odd social drink and a pint down the pub. Definitely one of life's pleasures! But perhaps my days of drinking more than this are over − and perhaps that is not such a bad thing!

LISTEN TO THE MUSIC

Sit back and listen to the music – no really, listen.

> *Music expresses that which cannot be put into words and that which cannot remain silent.*
>
> Victor Hugo

> *Music is the weapon of the future.*
>
> Various

> *Music is to the soul what words are to the mind.*
>
> Various

I have listened to the radio almost all my life, some news channels but mostly music. I like music. When Spotify came along and I could access any music, any time, I was like a kid in a candy shop.

The power of music is undeniable. To be more specific, the power of the right music at the right time is, to me, like no other tonic. Music can make 100,000 people dance together in a field, me and my family dance in the living room or put a smile on an individual's face as they listen through their headphones.

As a solution to my moods, music is massively powerful. It can both jolt me out of a bad mood and make an already good mood even better. We all have our own "go to" bands or songs. No one person is right or wrong. I guess it's like wine – it's personal taste. Some songs have stayed with me throughout my life. Some albums are deep in my psyche. The first few seconds of a single song can conjure up vivid memories from years ago.

Music can have its limits as a solution. When you are feeling in a dark place, a single song can block out what little light you have; an uplifting song can make you feel nothing. Too much music can also fill and crowd my brain. At times like these, I need a break from music; when music just becomes more than just background noise, I find it can increasingly be annoying rather than beneficial.

More and more, I find that I need to listen carefully to a song for it to have the most benefit. If it is just another distraction it loses its value. I guess really listening to music is the mindfulness or almost meditative part of listening – being truly in that moment and immersing yourself in that song – then the value is amplified.

Despite its limitations, I know that a well-chosen track from the right artist at the right time can be immensely powerful. When you have time to focus on it, to really listen, and you can play it really LOUD and uninterrupted, it can really change your mood. Try it.

Long may the magical and powerful effect of music remain for me.

DANCE TOGETHER

Dance together, cycle backwards and make soup.

I think, like many people, I have become set in my ways and a bit stale. I knew (or thought I knew!) what I enjoyed. I was comfortable with that knowledge and those activities. What was probably lacking in my life though was an ability or willingness to open up to other activities. Some will be brand new activities. But they also don't necessarily have to be new activities, but perhaps ones that I enjoyed in the past and which, for one reason or another, I had neglected as other parts of my life took over – work, family, other commitments and just everyday life.

I have analysed this a bit more closely and realized that there are some key things that I need to do more of again.

Different activities, which will benefit both me and others

I am now more open to different activities. Previously, I used to politely decline an offer to try something new; now, I try to say "yes".

So what if I am rubbish at something, or it's not really my thing? Having a go will get me thinking differently and doing different things.

Sometimes I now try and do my usual activities in a different way, to grow my "plasticity". For example, I reversed my usual cycling and running routes so that I would see the same things from the opposite direction – and it made a difference! So simple, but when I was set on my previous path I would do it so rarely or not at all. It was easy to just keep doing exactly what I was doing before.

As the master of very basic cookery skills, I would rarely do more than the bare minimum in the kitchen. In the weeks after my episode, I made soup! "Weird," I thought. "So what!" thinks the rest of the population who are more adventurous and able in the kitchen. But it was different, vaguely creative and produced something that others could enjoy as well.

Fun and engaging activities

This is a generic proposal, but as a general rule I think that as we get older, we have less fun, and flit from one thing or task to another so we are less engaged in what we do.

We may struggle to see the fun/engaging aspects of different activities and to engage with any such activities going on around us.

For me, for now, the solution should be that I should be open to more fun/engaging things out there. If the choice arises to either do something that *may* be fun/engaging or to carry on doing what I always do, then I think I should take the potentially fun option.

Socializing

There is some conflict here for me. I genuinely quite enjoy being on my own or with just my family. I rarely feel the urge to be involved in lots of social activities, and as such I have probably neglected and avoided some social situations.

I prefer to be around people I know well and in small groups, which sometimes limits my socialising opportunities. While I don't feel the need to go to the other extreme, I do think I should be open to, and probably be part of, organizing more social activities.

In the early days after my episode I stuck with the people I knew and in small groups, but in time I was able to expand to others and larger groups and got a massive benefit.

I now see the essential human need to interact and socialise, as well as the benefits of meeting brand new people and what enjoyment it gives me. I see the immense value of belonging and sharing. "No man is an island." But when I was feeling low I just couldn't see that. It all just seemed too hard.

Together time

I have lost count over the years of how many times my wife and I say we should spend more time together – time doing things other than daily, domestic stuff.

A real bonus of my post-episode time for reflection has been that I *have* spent more time with my wife – talking to her, walking together. This has been a real solace and opened up many magical moments.

We have always been close and spent time together, but it is easy for weeks to go by without us doing something together that is a bit different from the normality of married, family and home life. All those everyday activities are great, and provide the backdrop and anchor for our lives together, but they are even better if they are interspersed with other non-domestic and different activities.

The key now is to try and ensure that we continue to have these times together, away from the usual stuff, on a more frequent basis. To take the time to do different things with those close around.

THE ALGEBRA OF THE REASONS AND SOLUTIONS

Solutions x solutions or reasons x reasons. Combine them and the benefits multiply.

I kind of got maths at school – not all the time, and some just went over my head, but I got the basics. I understood multiplication and, at times, I even got algebra. It wasn't my strong point, but I used to occasionally suss out the value of x or y, and it felt like a revelation.

While writing this book, I have discovered that there is an interaction between the reasons for low moods and the solutions used to ease them. My theory loosely borrows a bit from multiplication and algebra, but it is more than that – it is more than the "whole being greater than the sum of its parts".

That is, reasons and solutions are related to each other; when a reason and/or a solution is combined with another reason or solution, their impact can be multiplied and magnified many, many more times than the individual parts.

Whatever the maths is, it doesn't really matter. Maybe it isn't even maths – maybe it's just common sense. What does matter is that there are spirals, both positive and negative – knock-on effects that can suddenly put you in a whole lot darker or brighter place than before.

Looking at the "reason" for my low moods at first, I see that one reason can have an impact on another reason; if one reason is present then it can have a knock-on impact on another reason. Suddenly, it isn't just one reason that is affecting your mood, it is two, or three, or more.

It's a downward spiral.

For example, one of my reasons for feeling low was because I felt I couldn't easily get away for either a short or long period. And getting away would mean spending money that I couldn't necessarily justify spending – creating another "reason" for my low moods.

The original "reason" was multiplied by a second reason.

On top of that, going away needed me to plan and commit (another "reason" for my low moods), rather than living "footloose and fancy free".

Suddenly, boom... reason one multiplied by reason two multiplied by reason three... The low moods have taken over.

What I had originally thought was one reason behind my low mood was actually multiple reasons. The weight of one thing then turned into the weight of three or four negatives, all contributing to the spiral. The result? I felt even lower.

I can also see how the reasons and solutions sometimes interacted to make me feel worse.

When the low moods take over or I become ill or injured then I am denied certain solutions. For example, when ill I can't interact and socialise (a solution), I can't exercise (another solution) and I take in less sun (another solution). Suddenly the low moods have snowballed.

However, crucially the same "multiplier" effect can work with solutions. Some solutions are like a magic medicine that you take once but which heals multiple illnesses; they are single solutions or activities but they have multiple benefits. These are the "money" or "killer" solutions I talked of earlier – the "silver bullets".

For example, running is an exercise that releases the "happy chemicals", PLUS gives you time alone, PLUS gives you time to think, PLUS has meditative and mindful benefits, PLUS it makes you more tired, so you sleep better.

The real trick here for me seems to be to identify those reasons that are related to each other and which have a bigger negative combined effect than you may think. I need to focus on them and identify how to improve them or avoid them as much as I can. Avoiding illness and injury is key for me; it's not always possible and is often out of my control, but I can be aware of it.

In parallel, I need to identify those "silver bullets" – the solutions that have multiple benefits – and do them again and again!

For me, the top few "silver bullets" that seem to have real benefit include:

- exercise
- taking a break
- socializing
- meditation
- sleep

But these solutions vary over time and are dependent on the situation. And for everyone they will be different.

WORK AS A SOLUTION – WHAT DO I WANT FROM WORK?

In my early analysis of the challenges I was facing, work appeared high on the list. As I worked through the reasons behind my low moods, I realized that while work clearly wasn't the only contributing factor, it was a big part of my underlying stress which led to low moods. I was living with the constant knowledge that there was something fundamentally wrong or missing in my work life, and this spilled over to the rest of my life.

So, a large part of any solution had to contain a full and frank look at any work issues and how to resolve them.

I have long had a desire to spend my work time engaged in something that is more "me" – more meaningful, fulfilling and with a real sense of purpose. I have realized too that I need to rethink my attitude to work. Put it into perspective: remember that "it's only work" while continuing to provide an excellent service in whatever I choose to do.

In my research, I stumbled across, and then explored further, some very helpful, generic "fulfilling job" criteria that could help me discover what it is I want out of a job. The key is now to look forward and work out how I use what I learnt from this research so that it turns into genuine features of my future work – to benefit both me and the entity I work for by doing a great job. Here I focus on what I can do to assist me and then I should more naturally be able to do my job well.

There is of course a whole host of tools that people use to summarize and assess what genuinely fulfils them. Psychometric tests can be used to show people's natural strengths and weaknesses. Other tools can come up with some overarching "job types" that may match people's interests and skills. These can be very useful and worth the investment

– I myself have done these in the past. But it is often then hard to convert that information into specific jobs that are available to you, are in your local area, and will earn you a living that is sustainable.

My intention in this next section is to add some thoughts to complement some of these tools I mention.

I take a simplistic approach, which can help to make you pay attention to what is important to you, to what specific characteristics of a job (rather than generic "job types") may resonate with you and, crucially, to your approach to work.

I then elaborate on the various "criteria" or principles for a fulfilling job; this process has made these principles more meaningful for me and have helped to clarify what I want from a job.

I had to give my work situation some serious thought, and I found some interesting theories out there. The best bit, however, was that there was not really anything especially difficult or new to grasp. So why had I missed it before now? I am still not sure, but I was probably just caught up in doing a job that I had fallen into other than really thinking it through.

I didn't find the various summaries of "most satisfying" jobs particularly helpful. I am sure there is merit in these "league tables" of the "best" jobs, and they are evidence-based, but despite being open minded, I was unlikely to become a clergyman (often put as number one for "most satisfying jobs")!

In my research I came across a summary of the "six qualities of highly satisfying jobs".[3] This seemed more useful. If I could recognize these qualities (or lack of them) in my current job, then I could make some changes to achieve them in a future role. Perhaps. Well, I could at least try.

I had always thought one should "follow one's passion" – and I still think that helps – but there seemed to be a school of thought that this could be limiting, and that your passion could be killed if it became your job. The "six qualities of highly satisfying jobs" seemed to go beyond the old mantra of passion-following.

---

3   Source: blog.rescuetime.com based on a University of Chicago study

The six qualities

I have added my own thoughts in italics to the list I read, which I try
and explain later.

- **Work that is engaging (*either effortlessly or with a
  proportionate amount of effort*).**
  This seems so simple and so true, so it has to be right up there –
  right at the centre of my quest for a more fulfilling role. But this on
  its own was too vague for me.

When I explored further, I read about "flow" – a word I had heard
and used before. "Flow" in this sense apparently means a task that
holds your attention, that just seems to (no great surprise) "flow"...
almost effortlessly – like a river flowing along. A job with flow is one
in which you are fully engaged and during which time just drifts by.

Some people have likened this to playing computer games, when
an hour can just flow by without one realizing. This analogy doesn't
directly work for me, but having witnessed my kids at the games
console, I do get it. And, as with jobs, many computer games also have
clear goals and defined start and end points.

I would probably say some engaging activity – like skiing down
a mountain – may be a better example for me... shame I don't get
to do it that much, and it doesn't seem to pay too well (at my
level anyway).

I have added *"either effortlessly or with a proportionate amount of effort"*
(although this contradicts a section later where I think the more effort
you put in brings the greater feeling of reward). But in this "quality" I
think that the effort and engagement need to have some correlation. Or,
even better, you can be genuinely engaged and "in the flow" without
necessarily putting in maximum effort.

To be honest, I can't sustain maximum effort the whole time at work
(or at most things). I can for periods, but it would be nice to "be in the
flow" and engaged even when (inevitably) some of my effort wanes a
little bit.

- **Work that benefits others (*and is something you believe in*).**
  This seems obvious – a task that results in direct and tangible
  benefit to others has the feel-good factor for everyone. Teaching,
  on paper, is a perfect example of this, and brings fulfilment
  to many.

I added *"is something you believe in"* because I think this is key; for
example, if I was teaching needlework I would get some fulfilment
from helping another person achieve something, but I would get
much more out of teaching something I really believe in – or is more
"me" – and from which I feel I can give and gain sustainable long-
term pleasure.

- **Work that you're good at (and feel valued for) *and have
  worked hard at to achieve in*.**
  When you are good at something you feel more comfortable,
  more relaxed and you know your skills are being put to good use.
  I remember someone once saying that there is great pleasure in
  watching someone who's really good at something, whatever it is.
  Whether it be an elite sportsman or a skilled bricklayer – there is
  a joy in seeing a skill mastered and then practised. So, if there is
  pleasure in the watching, I guess there is pleasure in the doing.
  I can see that this could go too far – for example, if you are so
  good at something you just do it on automatic pilot there is a risk
  you start to find it boring.
  I took the liberty of adding *"have worked hard at to achieve in."* I will
  need to test this further to see if it stands up to the test of time,
  but for now I maintain that there is more pleasure – sustainable
  and deeper pleasure – derived from something that has taken time
  to perfect. If things come too easily then they tend not to be as
  satisfying. The joy of doing something well after a lot of practice
  and effort tends to exceed the satisfaction gained from a skill that
  has been mastered quickly.
  And, if you take the joy of one's own effort to get to a place you
  are really good at, then if you are helping someone else to achieve
  this also, then surely that fulfilment is multiplied?

This isn't always true, and I think there is a "law of diminishing returns" here; for example, if something has taken absolutely ages to perfect, with many falls and heartache along the way, then the joy may have been eroded somewhat.

When you are valued for the thing you're good at, then it's an additional boost. It gives you a warm glow of satisfaction, of fulfilment. Whether that appreciation is shown by a genuine "thank you", or by the monetary reward that comes with paid work, this feeling of being valued is a vital element of fulfilment.

- **Flexibility in how and where you work (*and when*).**
  If you are constantly at the same desk, in the same office and having to work a number of core hours at specific times then I can see this would be less fulfilling than if you could be flexible as to where and when you worked.

  Having observed and taken part in flexible working, people often end up gravitating to a set location and routine anyway, but it's one they have chosen rather than had imposed upon them. They have made an active choice of location and timing. They are in control. They are more fulfilled.

  The advent of homeworking during the COVID pandemic (for the lucky ones who kept working and could work from home) put the joys, and let's be honest, some strains, of homeworking into the spotlight. Not everyone had more or full flexibility during this homeworking phase, but many did have more control over where and what hours they worked, compared to the more traditional office based, core hour model of working.

  I added "*when*" as I see this as key. I know people who work for themselves who get up at 5am and are all done by lunchtime. I am not sure that schedule is for me, but if you can find a timetable that works for you, I can see that being a real bonus.

- **A lack of major (*direct or indirect*) negatives.**
  This is a strange one at first glance. I guess we are mostly told to look at the positives and not the negatives in life. But the point here

seems to be that life and work are not perfect and therefore there will be downsides.

You have to accept these downsides, and just make sure that there aren't too many of them. Ideally, make sure that the negatives don't outweigh the positives.

A great example is the commute to work. If you have the most amazing job but it's at the end of a dreadful, long, tiring daily commute, then it's unlikely to be sustainable. That can be a major negative.

Sure, you could move to be nearer this amazing job, but perhaps financial or family commitments don't allow it. I see this barrier to improving the situation as an "*indirect*" negative, which I added. Another example could be a great job with annoying colleagues. Or a job that requires repeated weekend working, meaning you only rarely get quality family time.

I added "*direct or indirect*" because some negatives are directly associated with the actual job, such as irritating colleagues or the ridiculous rules you may have to adhere to at work. But as important are indirect negatives that may spread into your time out of work, such as the commute.

- **The chance for meaningful (*and productive and enjoyable*) collaboration.**

  As someone who tends to gravitate to working best alone, by cutting the world out and focusing on the task at hand, I don't immediately warm to this quality. But when I carefully consider my various previous jobs, I realize that I do thrive on collaboration – at the right time, with the right people and to a genuine shared goal. If I spend too much time working alone then I start to drift and eventually seek the company and input of others. And when I have worked with someone else or a team for a period of the day I have generally really enjoyed it.

  The addition of the word "meaningful" really makes this powerful, because someone else telling you what to do is *not* collaboration! I added the "*productive and enjoyable*" because, again, as with "meaningful", if you really get a buzz out of working in a team towards achieving a common goal then there are few greater feelings. And this applies to any team – that joy when a sports team scores is witnessed on sports grounds of every level around the world. And when a team scores a goal, that really is productive collaboration – "Wahey!"

I feel *"enjoyable"* is vital because if you can find like minded, positive, similarly minded "radiator" type people to collaborate with then the task at hand is a joy. Similarly if you have to work with colleagues that don't really want to be there, are not engaged and more like "sponges", then the collaboration can be stressful and unproductive at best; soul destroying at worst.

Me and my job(s) scored against the above criteria

So, now that I have plagiarised and heavily amended (and hopefully not weakened!) the good work of some respected academics, where do I, with my job and my best previous jobs, fit in to these criteria?

I thought it could be worthwhile to score some of my recent roles and what I perceive to be the best of my various previous jobs. That way I could understand why (or why not) some of these roles were not for me. Plus, rather than that potentially just being a negative exercise, I could look back and see when I had been happiest in work in the past and what I was doing at that time. From that, I could perhaps try and replicate some elements of that in the future.

I didn't want the specific details of my most recent jobs to be a major focus here as I felt that there was more value in looking at jobs overall rather than focusing on what was right or wrong for me in my specific recent roles.

Therefore, I haven't specifically scored previous jobs here, but if I were to score my jobs, I would use the following scale and complete the table below.

SCALE

- 1 = I would rather stab my eyes out/I will literally walk out at any minute.
- 10 = This is the best job ever and I would probably do this for no money because I get so much out of it.

CRITERIA FOR A FULFILLING JOB	CURRENT JOB SCALE 1-10	CURRENT JOB REASON FOR SCORE	BEST PREVIOUS JOB SCALE 1-10	PREVIOUS JOB – REASON FOR SCORE	CONCLUSION
Work that is engaging *(either effortlessly or with a proportionate amount of effort)*.					
Work that benefits others *(and is something you believe in)*.					
Work that you're good at *(and feel valued for) (and which you have worked hard to achieve in)*.					
Flexibility in how, and where you work *(and when)*.					
A lack of major *(direct or indirect)* negatives.					
The chance for meaningful *(productive and enjoyable)* collaboration.					

Give it a go with previous, current and importantly any potential future jobs. See how they score!

WORK AS A SOLUTION

The qualities detailed in the previous chapter are the principles that I feel are important to me for a fulfilling career.

As before in this book, I have sometimes used the first person in relation to work. But in reality, the thoughts are a culmination of mine and others' experiences – written from a single person's point of view but incorporating common threads that apply to so many jobs and careers in the 2020s.

The next task is to convert these principles into a real job description and job. In addition to any list of fulfilling criteria, there are clearly other considerations that come into play here. I have tried to capture the most important elements of a job and the employer/employee relationship. This clearly works best if you are "employed" in the traditional sense of the word, but it also works for the entrepreneurial and self-employed – there is still the link between the individual and what they do and for whom.

Money

There is the small issue of the money that I need or want to earn for a certain standard of living.

In an ideal world I wouldn't really need to earn as much as I do now and, as such, I could probably find a whole host of suitable jobs that would satisfy the above criteria and give me a fulfilling role. But, get real... money *is* a factor, and I need to take that into account.

However, I also need to be prepared to accept less money if the role is really right for me. I should "cut my cloth accordingly" and reduce expenditure where I can if it means I have a more satisfying, balanced and fulfilling life and job.

Skills

Another issue is the skills that I have now or can readily obtain through more training and experience.

Availability

Then there is the availability of jobs that fit my criteria where I currently live, or should I relocate to find that more fulfilling role?

A useful exercise to simplify some of this is to draw a Venn diagram with the following circles:

- my skills
- what's valued in society/in demand
- my passion/interest/fulfilment criteria

I should pursue a job in a profession that will cover the items that appear in the overlap.

Job success

An important factor is then actually getting the job! By that, I mean either convincing a potential employer or partner to take me on in the role I want – for mutual benefit. Or, for me to set myself up to actually carry out the role – to take the risk.

Honesty

I think another vital element I need is honesty. This came up as an earlier "general solution", as well as specifically in relation to work.

I need to be honest with myself and any future employer. It is easy to convince oneself that a particular role is right. The position may have a lot of positive features attached to it – such as being open now, near to where I live and paying the amount of money I need.

The real challenge is to be absolutely honest and true to myself so that I don't just *think* myself into a job. I need to be absolutely certain that I know that it *is* right for me.

In line with this, I need to make sure I avoid certain aspects in my next roles which I know are not really *me* and which do not give me satisfaction or create stress – things such as repetitive tasks, "an unprofessional environment", colleagues who see the work as a means to an end rather than something positive in which they believe and can really get involved.

Advice

I think that some third-party assistance from a good friend, colleague or family member is essential. I should discuss any new role with someone who knows and understands me. They can judge if I am just kidding myself about the suitability of a job, or if this is a genuine opportunity that will meet the criteria and ultimately provide me with a fulfilling role. This advice should aid the honesty process.

Advice

THE DREAM JOB

There are various ways of converting the principles and aspirations I have highlighted above into something more useful. One way is to write out a dream job description, listing all the things that I would really want to get from a role.

People may aspire to the "dream" job and perhaps it doesn't exist, but we can definitely aim high and try and achieve a much more fulfilling job at the very least. I want to strive for that, not mediocrity and killing time just counting the money coming in and wondering when I can go home.

It is important to be realistic, but I should also think big enough so that I don't just set myself up to do more of what I have already been doing, which has ultimately been unfulfilling and has led to where I am now!

I recently extended the "fulfilling job" criteria, which I listed before, to cover:

- Answers a genuine and pressing need
- Has direct visible benefits to others
- Is engaging, enjoyable, absorbing work
- Is work that I am good at and uses my existing skills
- Involves genuine, productive and enjoyable collaboration, as well as working alone
- Provides appropriate support from others
- Has targets that are achievable, realistic and appropriately resourced
- Offers flexibility
- Values and rewards my skills

Another way is to look at available jobs and use the table I set out earlier and the above criteria to rate each job description. No job will tick every box, but it can be a relative scale and it will give me a good idea of where I might have to compromise and also where I am not prepared to accept compromises.

My approach and attitude to work

Assuming that I succeed in building as many of my fulfilling criteria into a role, that is only part of the battle to being fulfilled at work.

Another crucial aspect is actually adopting the right approach and attitude to work. Improving my approach and attitude would *allow* me to be more fulfilled, and so better manage the inevitable stresses and strains of work.

Here are a few things that I think I need to work towards.

TALK, COLLABORATE AND CONSULT, BUT ALSO ACT

Collaboration is good and I need to "just do it".

If the work is answering a pressing need, then I need to make sure I get on with my part of achieving this pressing need. At the right point I need to make sure I take responsibility − assertively and politely − so the task progresses and gets completed. Ultimately, just get on with it.

TAKE TIME TO SEE THE RESULTS AND THE EFFECT OF THE WORK

I need to take more pleasure in the results − not dwell on them − just acknowledge how my work contributed to the overall results.

For example, if after a day of interviewing candidates for a position the result is someone has a job − a livelihood for them and their family − then I need to take some satisfaction that I have helped that process. My job that day will have benefitted others.

Equally I need to really understand the task at hand − if I clearly know what I am doing and why I am doing it then I enjoy it more. Ultimately I like to just "get things done" and to be allowed to do that.

ALLOW MYSELF TO BE ENGAGED AND ABSORBED

Some of my previous, less fulfilling roles, have brought on a natural reticence in me – a "what else could I be doing?" feeling. This flies in the face of the "live in the moment" attitude that I now understand is essential.

We all need some element of work to keep us busy, interested and pay the bills. So, I should apply the "acceptance of the inevitable" solution to work – accept I have to work, and just get on with it. Once I accept I am at work and focus on the moment, then I think I could allow myself to be more absorbed in a task; the more I am absorbed, the more I will be engaged. And, ultimately, as well as doing a much better job the more I could enjoy it.

I need to allow this to happen.

HAVE SELF-BELIEF

I need to feel more confident – and to truly believe it as well. The two go hand in hand, but are also separate.

I know I can do this, because someone else obviously thinks I can or they wouldn't have given me the job! I need to take pleasure in knowing that I can do the work. I may not be the best in the world at it, but I am the one doing it now.

I also need to embrace when I can't do something – be honest about it, seek out training, and learn.

TALK FIRST, EMAIL LATER

Take time to build relationships and then use them. Talk and catch up with others. Invest time in small talk.

I need to seek out more human interaction. It is easy to hide behind emails and written reports, and I think my previous roles almost encouraged this as email provides evidence of action. But it also produced a "blame culture" in a way – a "Well, it says here, in the email" kind of thinking. I found that a negative environment.

I need to talk more. Take time to talk about things. Chat more in the office (if I work in one!) and away from the office. Engage in more face-to-face talk if possible, but also on the phone. I think this will encourage better collaboration and more fulfilling interactions and work.

I have so many contacts; I need to reach out to them and work with them – and socialize with them. Having a "catch up" or some lunch can nourish social interaction and normally always comes out with a new approach or thought.

ACCEPT SUPPORT

Ask for help.

I need to ensure that I have the support I believe I need to succeed. I need to shout early on if there is a problem, or even before there is a problem if I can see issues potentially arising.

And if I am not happy with the support I receive, then I need to be honest and seek more and/or different support.

BE REALISTIC

I have a responsibility to ensure I have the right resources to achieve a reasonable objective. However, if a problem arises that is beyond my area of expertise, capacity or responsibility, and is therefore out of my control, then I need to worry less. Once I have done what I can to highlight and then rectify the problem I need to recognize that:

• it is not my fault
• I am going to work around it and be okay with what I do have
• I am not going to be blamed

I need to be assertive and polite enough to say "No" if faced with unrealistic demands. And to say it with some justification, minimal guilt, and then move on.

Where possible, I need to leave some space and time (headroom) to ensure that when an urgent task comes along I can deal with it. Or, even better, I will have time to "think outside the box" and think strategically. More time and space will allow for more strategic planning and less operational action, so I will be able to spend more time on the important, but not urgent tasks which I discussed earlier.

To do this, I need to take the time and seek support from others.

MIX IT UP

Go for a walk. Don't always work in the office. Turn up late now and again.

I need to grasp and take advantage of the flexibility I am afforded/ fought for. I don't think it needs to be a sea change, but I need to ensure I take a walk round the block occasionally to aid my thought processes.

I should be a bit more flexible in where I work – work from home, from a cafe, anywhere if appropriate and aids my productivity and improves the result.

Take the long cycle to work in the sunshine one morning so that I can be happier sitting inside. So what if I am a bit late now and again?! (As long as I don't let others down.) If I work flexibly, I can make the time up later and still complete the task.

MONEY IN THE BANK

At the end of the day, so far in my career I have managed to be paid a wage that has enabled me to meet my lifestyle. I have deliberately not always followed the money, but have sought out alternative routes so I could have been paid more, and I could probably be paid less. But ultimately, it is what it is. Live with it.

At the end of the day

Strive for excellence, not perfection. Think... "I did that and it's a job well done."

Life isn't perfect, and neither is work. Even a job that requires you to perform close to perfection is, I doubt, performed perfectly. There are normally some tolerances or margins for error. Perfection is impossible, but excellence will get the job done. And excellence will give me pride and fulfilment.

Remember that it's just a job. Learn to let things go and to care less. Ultimately, work is just work. Most people "work to live" and not the other way round. Put it in perspective – no one person is indispensable. The world carries on.

I do care and I always will, but I need to detach myself more at the right times. I am not responsible for everything and I need to trust and work with others so everyone pulls their weight.

Work happens at work; I need to make sure it is just one element of my life and that I have the time to enjoy plenty of other things – family, hobbies, sitting in the sunshine, whatever.

Now for action

So, now I need to actually embark on this process. At least I have a process now – some criteria for a fulfilling job and a new approach – and I definitely have a need and a real desire to put this into action.

FINAL THOUGHTS

I have covered various solutions here which I found to be a good starting point to help me through this difficult time. Equally, there will no doubt be a whole set of other potentially helpful solutions I have spectacularly missed out. Just like when you review a document, you focus on what is there rather than what isn't.

For example, I have made no mention of medications, such as sleeping pills, antidepressants or similar. The truth is, as I have no experience of these I do not feel able to comment.

Medication was discussed with my doctor, and they were part of my research, but on balance I always wanted to try the other solutions first: counselling, on-line help, talking, meditation, etc. These solutions also seemed to be readily and quickly available, and I hoped to combine them with time to allow them to work.

The reality is also that I may not have been so low as to require any medication. Who knows? But I do know that, so far, I have been able to feel better without medication. But for others this may not be the case and whether people consider any medication are individual decisions to be taken with the appropriate medical advice.

I wonder if the propensity to these moods is a little like having back pain or a similar recurring injury. Once you have had back pain, for many, it doesn't ever really go away. You are given exercises and stretches to do, which you engage with while the pain is real or recent. These help reduce the symptoms and pain, and then you feel better and the risk is that you slacken up on the exercises and stretches. And, guess what? The back pain returns.

In a similar way, I can see that my solutions here will need to be in place on an almost permanent basis. That is why I focused on what

I thought were sustainable solutions – things I could build into my life. Sure, I will neglect some solutions – that's only human. But, if my personal barometer starts to show a sign that the low moods are returning, I will be able to use my findings in this book as a way of reminding me to focus on the solutions once more.

As I went through my journey, I genuinely felt like a walking cliché. Too many clichés annoy most people, but I get the reason behind them – they are so true. Here are just a few of my favourites which seemed to ring true in those few months.

- "I feel a bit up and down." Wow that one did my head in, but it was so true it wasn't funny; I pretty much always feel up and down!
- "A problem shared is a problem halved." Talk to others and you feel better.
- "It's good to get it off your chest." Again, talk and share.
- "It's only a phase." It will get better.
- "In time, it too shall pass." Again, bad situations will improve and vice versa.

And there are hundreds more! Each of these clichés reminded me that I am not alone, that others had gone through similar feelings and patterns before, and this realization was a solution in itself.

PART FOUR
CONCLUSIONS

EVERY CLOUD HAS A SILVER LINING

It may seem strange to think that there are areas of your life that may actually improve and get better as a direct result of having a propensity for low moods, or from having an episode, as I did. After a period of reflection and the introduction of new strategies and habits in my life, I can see there were many positives to be gained from having gone through this dark period.

Be under no illusion, when you are feeling very low you cannot see or feel much apart from that horrible, negative, doubtful vulnerability and lowness. But I did also feel from the beginning that this was an opportunity to discover things about myself and hopefully work out a better way of living for myself, so that I could cope better with life's ups and downs – to benefit myself, my family and all those around me.

For myself, there have been many benefits directly as a result of this period in my life.

For example, I should hopefully be able to recognise in any future low times that this will indeed pass, and that I can be more peaceful with and caring towards myself.

Ultimately, I will be able to put into practice these solutions so that those lower moods are hopefully less deep and less frequent. I may not be able to stop all the low moods (who can?), but if I can reduce them, then when the odd low mood does occur, I will recognise it and increase my measures and solutions to counteract it. That will be a huge benefit.

I know people sometimes say, "If you don't feel the lows then you can't really feel the highs", or, "It's only through sinking so low that you get to reach those high points." And I kind of get that philosophy.

I can also see that some people are perhaps less sensitive to emotions than others – they may not feel those low lows and, perhaps as a result, they don't feel the high highs. Instead, they just "are" – in one constant(ish) state. I have never really been like that, so I can't really judge them, envy them or pity them. It's just not me.

I guess, if I get those emotional highs – those really amazing and good days, those truly happy times when life really is magical and the roses smell *that* good – then there is a theory that these good feelings are enhanced because at other times I know those depths – the depths of low moods. I think that theory should be appreciated.

The other benefit to me is the self-learning process I have been through. It has been intense and difficult, but I have learnt so much about myself, about others and about the life we all share on this little planet. To have had the reason, the catalyst, the time, the opportunity and the need to have delved deep into this subject generally and specifically, with me and my feelings at the centre, has been a real privilege and a worthwhile experience.

Crucially, my interaction with others close to me has, I think, seen vast, if perhaps still inconsistent, improvement. My understanding, sympathy and empathy for people with other challenges has grown hugely. I know to look beyond the symptom in almost everyone's behaviour, to seek out the root cause and to then be more understanding.

Previously, I may have been wrapped up in my own life and dismissed peoples' concerns or worries as not really being valid. I now know that if they are valid to that person then that makes them very real, potentially life-changing and far from trivial. I understand that there is a cause for their issues, even if I don't necessarily understand the cause itself.

I think that my experience has given me a greater desire to understand others' issues and to give them the space, opportunity and (more often than not) a sounding board/sympathetic ear for them to offload on, which enables me to start to understand their challenges.

In turn, I am much more open to and understanding of other peoples' moods or actions within their own life which, although may not be "my cup of tea", may be very important to them. As a result,

I now have much more understanding of the way different people "cope" or choose to "thrive".

A good example of this, although I now look back and cringe at my own insensitivity and lack of understanding, is other peoples' needs for regular catch ups. I used to look a bit unsympathetically at the "coffee and a chat" or the regular "girls' night out", instead seeing it as time that they could be doing something constructive. Oh, how I now cringe with embarrassment at my own lack of understanding of what makes people tick. How that human need for belonging, sharing, talking and feeling part of something bigger than the individual is an instinctive human emotion and desire – one that needs to be nourished, not neglected.

But also I know I was not alone with these feelings. I know of husbands and wives who frequently clash because the husband can't understand his wife's need for *another* coffee morning or time to do something else with someone else! I now look at people who have these regular social interactions and genuinely think, "Good for you." They seem to have sussed out what a lot of people (a generalization here – sorry – men especially) have yet to discover – the need for this interaction – those that practise this are the sensible ones and they are reaping the benefits.

Importantly, I think that there have also been benefits for others who I really don't have much to do with – that stranger in the street or colleague at work. Not only do I hope to be more understanding of their issues, but I would hope that as a result of actively putting into practice some of the solutions I have identified, I will be a more balanced, more patient and ultimately better person to be around.

And if, at times I find it hard to be that better person, the very fact that I am now more aware of the need to be better will, I believe, be of benefit to others.

I also hope that the sharing of my experiences and thoughts on some solutions through this book may help others. Mental health and wellbeing is talked about more and more frequently and that has to be a good thing. But it still has a long way to go so that everyone who suffers from similar challenges has the confidence to be honest without the judgment of others. It has a long way to go to be fully understood. In my experience there is still some stigma and a reluctance to admit to it for fear of ramifications.

What will people think of me? Am I failing? Will an employer still employ me? Do I want others to know the depths of some of my inner thoughts?

I have grappled with all of these questions before this book was published. Some people counselled against publishing. But overwhelmingly I think it is vital to be honest, to acknowledge who we are and crucially to put a head above a parapet in the hope that others may benefit from knowing that they are not alone. So that those others know that such feelings are normal and significantly, to know that they will feel better. Life <u>will</u> improve.

IT'S JUST A PHASE

When we had our first child, I used to enjoy the various baby books that welcomed the uninitiated to the world of parenting. One piece of advice has always stayed with me from one of the better books.

"It's just a phase."

It was said in relation to any phase in a newborn's life. Various phases included: when the baby doesn't sleep, when they cry, when they scream because of teething, when they throw food at you, when they scream at being left alone, when they punch, kick, bite. All the great phases of stress as the baby grows into a toddler and then to the next stage again.

During any of these phases, the situation is bad. The relentlessness. The sleepless nights. The whole giant realization that this is your life and you've got to deal with it. But among all those challenges and the self-doubt of the new parent, the book reminds you that all of these "are just phases." Both the good and the not so good.

So, remember, whatever it is, however hard it is at the time, however low you feel, it will pass.

It really is just a phase.

In a similar way, as I have alluded to throughout this book, the low moods are similar – they are just a phase and they do lift and pass. I knew this before my episode, but right in the thick of my lowest period, I definitely couldn't believe it. When I was at my lowest, I really thought that this was it – "This is me and this is how I am always going to be." It was very, very tough.

I now tell myself it's just a phase and it will pass. But it's the hardest thing to see and believe when you are in a low place. Never underestimate how low people can feel and how they genuinely do not believe that anything will improve. No matter what others think, say or how they may act.

Similarly, above the clouds there is always blue sky. Granted, when you're stuck in or beneath those dark, foreboding clouds, it doesn't feel like it. At the time it can be so hard, almost impossible, to see beyond, but the sun is there and, at various times and sometimes just briefly, the clouds do lift and the sun does again reveal itself.

I do think that there are activities that can help make this process of seeing the blue sky happen more quickly. These activities are the potential solutions that have been at the front of my mind over the last few months and which now appear in this book.

Often just the passing of time will be essential.

These solutions may also help prevent the moods in the first place.

A favourite term from a work colleague is, "Shit rolls downhill. And I live in a valley." It can certainly feel like that for all of us at times – at work and in life in general. But, perhaps some of the solutions I have suggested can assist the process of trying to move out of that valley before the shit starts rolling down towards you.

It may take time to climb those valley sides, and you may end up rolling or falling back down time and time again, but overall, it's worth having a go at doing something about that shit-filled, valley life. Have a go at seeing if it's possible to head to the mountain top, or at least the foothills now and again.

Even before the low moods have taken hold, as well as during the dark times, some perspective is always needed. To achieve that perspective, I try to both metaphorically and physically get above those dark clouds. Perhaps by climbing a hill on a day when the valley is filled with cloud, but the summit is under blue skies. Or when on an aeroplane I will look out of the window, maybe with my favourite song playing through my headphones. The clouds are below, the blue sky is all around and above me the sun is shining.

On these occasions, my home, my life, my problems and my challenges are just a little dot below. Still there, but in proportion and not as overwhelming. This perspective doesn't always last. You walk back down the hill or the flight ends. But for those moments when I am up there looking at that blue sky, I know the metaphorical clouds in my mind will also lift. And eventually they do – the clouds lift and the blue sky and sunshine fills us with that lightness that, as human beings, we know as life, or if we are lucky enough, and after a lot of hard work, as happiness.

THE COVID-19 CONCEPTION

This book was conceived and born during one of modern man's most momentous, far-reaching and life-changing periods. The impact of the coronavirus on all areas of our lives, including our mental wellbeing, has been widely documented... and the true, long-lasting effects are yet to be discovered and truly understood.

But if this book was my "COVID-19 baby", the actual reasons for my low moods were *not* due to the coronavirus. I know this because my symptoms occurred before the pandemic was taking hold. The full extent of what was then being classed as an epidemic was only just emerging as I dealt with my own personal challenges. The original episode that prompted me to write this book occurred a few weeks before the first COVID-19 case was found. What a lifetime ago that feels. How the world has changed – in a macro sense for the global population and in a micro sense for all of us, including me.

I find this small but clear time separation – just a handful of weeks between my episode and the start of the outbreak – both interesting and helpful. As a result, I can safely say that the pandemic was not one of the initial triggers or reasons for my low feelings, for the simple fact that *it didn't actually exist* on that fateful day when I bought the router and had the significant dissociation episode. So if it didn't exist on the day of my episode then it certainly didn't exist in the weeks and months beforehand, which were when the root causes of my own challenges really started to take hold.

However, the initial weeks and then months of my recovery and return to normality took place with COVID-19 as a constant backdrop in the media, as the world witnessed what was about to unfold. As I write now, just before publishing, the coronavirus has marauded through almost every country, affecting every person's life on our little planet. Its effects have been widespread: it has maimed, killed, ruined personal and national economics, closed borders and impacted on almost every facet of our lives.

The widespread effect on mental health of this bizarre and intriguing period, which almost every person in the world will learn about or remember firsthand, has been widely discussed in the media. This has also shone a spotlight at the very heart of many of the topics in this book, including my experiences: the reasons for why I sometimes feel low, and the solutions to help me feel better. Looking at it as positively as possible, almost everything that I have included in this book is more readily understood, covered in the media and crucially, is discussed much more openly than it ever has been before. As these issues have affected so many more people, in turn, those people can now benefit from understanding and practising the sustainable solutions that I discuss in the book.

The coronavirus and its drastic effect on the lives of many have also helped put my episode and recovery into perspective. In the grand scheme of things, I feel fortunate. Overall, and compared to many, I was doing just fine. At least that is how I feel now – with some time and space after my episode – and how I started to feel when I was well on the road to feeling better. However, it was definitely not how I felt in the early weeks. I have to admit that at my worst, I dismissed the effects and seriousness of COVID-19. This was partly because I was so low, I didn't have the capacity to consider other issues. I was too busy worrying about myself and my own recovery rather than considering the lives of other people. But this was also because it is only with hindsight that we now know that almost everyone, including me, underestimated the seriousness of the pandemic.

As the world got to grips with and understood the gravity of the pandemic, by pure good timing and through me implementing my own solutions in my life, I started to feel better. I was learning how to process and deal with these feelings and I had found strategies to help me. It is so interesting and positive for me to see many of the solutions I cover in this book discussed so widely in the media to assist others who have been suffering with their own challenges. It also gave me the confidence to really believe in the value of the solutions I had discovered – and which I had tailored to suit me.

Although my solutions are not coronavirus-specific, I do believe that many of my proposed solutions can help people suffering from different forms of mental health challenges, including those that are affecting so many due to COVID-19, namely (at the time of writing) anxiety about emerging on the other side of the pandemic. On a basic level, these include the need for connection with others and the importance of routine, exercise and balance, which are all covered in my suggested solutions.

The coronavirus and the attendant lockdowns did, of course, create so many issues. The restrictions of people's freedom; the loneliness; the hours and days inside; the lack of human contact; the reduction in people's ability to practise hobbies; the increase in domestic violence. The sad list of negative consequences due to the coronavirus is a long one. These are just some of the challenges it brought with it, which were probably not really covered in my own personal "reasons" for my low feelings. And thank goodness for that. However, many of its issues do have similarities to some of my experiences. The feeling of frustration; the lack of control over my future; the feeling of being trapped; financial worries; the inability to get away from home.

The solutions clearly have massive parallels. As the coronavirus took hold I was so thankful for my recent experiences. I felt much more prepared to deal with the mental health fallout from the pandemic. This was for the simple reason that I was already practising many of my solutions. I'd had a "dry run" or a practice in real-time, with real consequences and real feelings. It was a very difficult dry run to go through but it was massively beneficial to me as I lived through 2020 and 2021, newly equipped with a "mental health toolkit" to help me cope better.

My experience armed me with exactly the right tools at exactly the right time to face the emerging mental health challenges. The coronavirus was never going to come along at the "right time" but if it had to happen at any time in my life I am thankful that it happened just after my episode. If it happened just a few months earlier I think the depths of my low moods would have been far deeper and in turn,

I would not have had the tools to deal with and help me emerge from those depths.

Although I had some of the right tools, I also know I was not immune to the mental health effects of COVID-19. I went through many of the similar challenges that so many people endured. The pause on normal life that the pandemic imposed on us all has probably also delayed a fuller and more comprehensive mental health recovery. But equally, this enforced pause has brought some significant advantages for me as I was more able to put my solutions and strategies in place in a slightly different time and a different world.

So hopefully, as the world learns to live and adjust in the immediate aftermath of the pandemic, I have more strength, better strategies and improved inner confidence, which will enable me to cope much better. I hope everyone who reads this can finish it feeling the same way.

Mat Desforges, 2021

ACKNOWLEDGEMENTS

I always like to hear others' views and am open to people's thoughts and wisdom. As a result, I am indebted to many people for their wise words, far beyond those mentioned here.

Long before I started this book a good friend and his then girlfriend told me, "The hardest thing about writing a book is starting it." True. Thanks to Tim and Jane I made the effort to start this in the first place. And they were positive and supportive once they heard about the book.

I found writing this book was a very personal undertaking which just meant me and a laptop, alongside some peace and quiet on my bike or a walk as I marshalled the mushy thoughts in my head. Parallel to that process, I leant on others and this is where the thanks and acknowledgments are due, to a small but important group of close confidants.

Al, Chris, Ed P, Darcy and Jason provided varied and valued input. Al was the first person, apart from my wife, who read the original manuscript and provided objective advice and gave me the confidence to work with publishers. Jason is normally the first person I go to with either very good or very bad news and he is always there to talk things through.

Chris was there for me right from the start of this journey – helping and suggesting – he was invaluable.

In the final stages of the book (and once I told them I was writing one!) my family, including Dan, Emma, Jonah and my parents, were really supportive, interested and helpful offering suggestions and comments. Thanks to Laura for her immediate support with one key chapter.

The team at my publisher have been excellent. They have been patient, helpful, professional and always available. A special thanks goes to Jess, Kayleigh, Rachel… and Kate, whose skilful editing worked magic on my "eats, shoots and leaves" grammatical errors and made sense of what I was trying to say.

Further thanks go to a number of my close family/friends and also distanced acquaintances, who were there for me during this difficult period. They listened, talked and provided support. It was all of you who got me through this time and this book, making me realize that I was not alone and tough times and mental challenges are normal, common, understandable and ultimately something we can all deal with.

My final thanks goes to my amazing and lovely wife, Ali and our two sons. Ali for always being there – whatever, and whenever. And my sons for providing grounding, reality, enthusiasm and a window to another world.

ABOUT THE AUTHOR

Mat Desforges is a dad, husband, brother, son, friend, acquaintance. Just like many of us are or will be.

Mat grew up in Dorset and was educated there as well as in Devon and France before moving to London and Guernsey after university. He then travelled and worked abroad before settling back in Guernsey for many years with his wife and now his two sons.

He has worked in a variety of roles in the commercial sector, government and regulation.

At the time of publishing, he is travelling with his family on what the kids have called a "global family adventure." This pause from normal family life was partly inspired by the experiences he recounts in *Down... but NOT Out,* his first book. While away he is working on a second book.

ABOUT CHERISH EDITIONS

Cherish Editions is a bespoke self-publishing service for authors of mental health, wellbeing and inspirational books.

As a division of Trigger Publishing, the UK's leading independent mental health and wellbeing publisher, we are experienced in creating and selling positive, responsible, important and inspirational books, which work to de-stigmatize the issues around mental health and improve the mental health and wellbeing of those who read our titles.

Founded by Adam Shaw, a mental health advocate, author and philanthropist, and leading psychologist Lauren Callaghan, Cherish Editions aims to publish books that provide advice, support and inspiration. We nurture our authors so that their stories can unfurl on the page, helping them to share their uplifting and moving stories.

Cherish Editions is unique in that a percentage of the profits from the sale of our books goes directly to leading mental health charity Shawmind, to deliver its vision to provide support for those experiencing mental ill health.

Find out more about Cherish Editions by visiting cherisheditions.com or by joining us on:

Twitter @cherisheditions
Facebook @cherisheditions
Instagram @cherisheditions

Cherish
EDITIONS

ABOUT SHAWMIND

A proportion of profits from the sale of all Trigger books go to their sister charity, Shawmind, also founded by Adam Shaw and Lauren Callaghan. The charity aims to ensure that everyone has access to mental health resources whenever they need them.

You can find out more about the work Shawmind do by visiting their website: shawmind.org or joining them on

Twitter @Shaw_Mind
Facebook @ShawmindUK
Instagram @Shaw_Mind